# PROBLEMS AND THEORIES
# OF PHILOSOPHY

*by*
*Kazimierz Ajdukiewicz*

*Translated by*
**Henryk Skolimowski**
*Department of Humanities,*
*University of Michigan*
*and*
**Anthony Quinton**
*Fellow of New College, Oxford*

CAMBRIDGE UNIVERSITY PRESS
CAMBRIDGE
LONDON · NEW YORK · MELBOURNE

Published by the Syndics of the Cambridge University Press
The Pitt Building, Trumpington Street, Cambridge CB2 1RP
Bentley House, 200 Euston Road, London NW1 2DB
32 East 57th Street, New York, NY 10022, USA
296 Beaconsfield Parade, Middle Park, Melbourne 3206, Australia

Library of Congress catalogue card number: 72–97878

hard covers ISBN: 0 521 20219 1
paperback ISBN: 0 521 09993 5

First published 1973
First paperback edition 1975

First printed in Great Britain
by W. & J. Mackay Limited, Chatham
Reprinted at the
University Printing House, Cambridge
(Euan Phillips, University Printer)

# Contents

# Translators' Preface

## Philosophy and logic in modern Poland

One of the most remarkable national contributions to learning of this century is the logic and philosophy produced in
Poland, particularly during its two decades of genuine independence. Logic, in its modern, mathematical form, is less
disadvantaged than philosophy if expressed in a little-known
language, since the proportion of straightforward prose in it
is comparatively small. Furthermore, logical works of the
greatest importance are often quite short and so offer no
great obstacle to translation. As a result the logicians of
modern Poland, in particular the three great Polish masters of
the discipline in recent times, Lukasiewicz, Lesniewski and
Tarski, are well known to the philosophers and logicians of
the rest of the world.★

The philosophy associated with this powerful and produc-
tive school of logic is less familiar. But Polish logic originated
from philosophy in the first place in the sense that its foun-
ders, Lukasiewicz and Lesniewski, came to the subject from

---

★ See *Polish Logic*, edited by Storrs McCall, Clarendon Press,
Oxford, 1967, which contains historical surveys by Kotarbinski and Jordan as well as seventeen logical papers.

philosophy and were both pupils of the philosopher Twardowski, whose teaching was the starting-point of this entire movement of thought. Furthermore, the work of the two leading Polish philosophers of the twentieth century, Kotarbinski and Ajdukiewicz (the author of this book), stands in a close relation to formal logic in much the same way as logic and philosophy are connected in the writings of Frege, Russell, Carnap and Quine.

Twardowski himself was a pupil of the Austrian philosopher, Franz Brentano, along with Husserl and Meinong. His approach to philosophy was, like theirs, of a broadly phenomenological character in that it took the form of an exact scrutiny of the precise introspectible nature of mental and, in particular, intellectual processes. Brentano had assigned to philosophy the task of investigating, not the causes and effects, the regular physical and physiological accompaniments, of such processes, but the intrinsic structure of the processes themselves. Together with that of Husserl and Meinong, Twardowski's own work was concerned with the nature of thought, whose articulation into acts, contents and objects he carefully analysed.

It was not, however, either the rather narrowly mental subject-matter or the phenomenological procedure of Twardowski that underlay the great creative influence he had on logic and philosophy in Poland, although those aspects of his work were directly continued by the distinguished phenomenologist, Roman Ingarden. His influence flowed, first, from his personal, patriotic decision to carry on his professional career not, as he could easily have done, at the Austrian centre of the Habsburg empire but at its outer limits in Lwow (in the south-east of Poland and now incorporated in the Soviet Union), and, secondly, from the remarkable and irresistible example he gave (in this strictly Polish location) of absolute clarity and precision of thought. His marvellously lucid and rigorous style of thinking, in which all crucial terms are explicitly defined or explained and all inferences set out so that their logical structure is absolutely perspicuous was firmly imparted to his pupils, and it has remained a persisting feature of Polish logic and philosophy. Those pupils soon fell under the influence of Russell and Whitehead's *Principia Mathematica*. The main lines of Russell's logical work had been laid down before he became aware that they had been anticipated in the much more rigorous, but hitherto almost wholly neglected, writings of Frege. The Polish logicians, particularly Lesniewski, were conscious of Frege from the beginning, with beneficial consequences for the quality of their work.

In this way the leading philosophers of Poland came to adopt a position about the correct method of philosophy similar to that of the analytic philosophers of western Europe and the United States, which takes the prime business of philosophy to be the investigation of thought in the shape of an analysis of it in its linguistically explicit form, the analysis itself being carried on with the principles of definition and inference specified by formal logic. Like the Wittgenstein of the *Tractatus* they took philosophy to be 'the logical clarification of thoughts'. It is a style of philosophising that nowhere outside Poland, except perhaps in the writings of Carnap, so thoroughly achieves its ideal of austerely impersonal diction, of freedom from any taint of the subjective, the literary and the emotional.

Like the logical positivists of the Vienna Circle the leading philosophers of modern Poland found in modern formal logic an instrument of analysis that would allow philosophy to become truly scientific. Kotarbinski, indeed, dissented from the anti-metaphysical insistence of the logical positivists. Like Quine more recently, he has always taken the view that ontology, the determination of the main kinds of entity that really exist, is a proper and central part of philosophical inquiry. Ajdukiewicz was closer to Carnap and the positivists, although, as this book shows, less hostile than all of them but Schlick to the idea that the logically renovated philosophy of the present day is continuous with the philosophical work of the past.

## Ajdukiewicz's life

Kazimierz Ajdukiewicz was born in December 1890 in Tarnopol, in Galicia. His parents moved, first to Cracow, where he attended the high school, and then to Lwow, where he attended the university, studying philosophy as his main subject under Twardowski and also working in mathematics and physics. His knowledge of logic began with his attendance at the lectures of Lukasiewicz. In 1912 he obtained his doctorate with a dissertation on Kant's theory of the *a priori* nature of space and left Lwow for further study at Göttingen, where Hilbert, the great mathematician and formalistic philosopher of mathematics, was teaching, as also was Husserl.

In the 1914–1918 war he served in the army on the Austro-Italian front, was decorated for bravery for rescuing some comrades from a ruined fort and was finally demobilised in 1920 with the rank of captain. Soon after he became professor of philosophy at the university of Warsaw and married the daughter of his teacher Twardowski. In 1928 he returned to Lwow as professor and remained there during the war, for some of the time teaching physics in a technical school. After the expulsion of the Germans from Poland in 1944 and the reconstitution of the Polish state under Russian auspices he was appointed professor of logic and the philosophy of science at the university of Poznan, where he remained until 1952, serving as rector of the university during his last four years there.

From 1954 until his death in 1963 he lived in Warsaw. Until his retirement at the age of seventy in 1960 he was head of the institutes of logic at both the university of Warsaw and the Polish Academy of Science. He remained until his death the chief editor of *Studia Logica*, the periodical in which logical and logico-philosophical works by Polish thinkers were published in more generally accessible languages: English, French, German and Russian.

Between 1948 and 1954 the communist regime in Poland, having successfully eliminated all effective political opposition, extended its attention to embrace the less immediately dangerous aspects of culture which it found unacceptable as residues of bourgeois liberalism. The logically oriented philosophy of the inter-war period came under heavy attack. It should be said that this attack was primarily intellectual. The exponents of bourgeois philosophy, with their anti-dialectical hostility to contradictions, were vehemently criticised but, although in many cases forbidden to teach, or to publish anything but translations of classic philosophical works, they were not in general deprived of academic employment or subjected to the full ferocity of 'administrative pressure'. That fate was largely reserved for dissident Marxists.

Ajdukiewicz was singled out for specially intense polemical treatment at the hands of Adam Schaff, the member of the central committee of the ruling party with particular responsibility for ensuring the dominance of the orthodox faith in the intellectual and cultural field. In 1952 Schaff published a long essay in which Ajdukiewicz's philosophy was indicted for 'idealism' in virtue of its alleged ascription of an autonomous, and therefore spiritual, existence to language in its picking out of language as the primary object of philosophical investigation. Ajdukiewicz was allowed to publish a reply of comparable length the following year, that of Stalin's death. From 1955 onwards he was able to resume the publication of his philosophical opinions in a non-defensive way.

Ajdukiewicz published eight books and a great number of articles, more than fifty of which are brought together in the two volumes of *Język i Poznanie* (*Language and Cognition*), vol. I, 1960, vol. II, 1965. Some of these articles are to appear in English translation in a volume to be published by D. Reidel and Co. Ajdukiewicz's books are: *On the Methodology of the Deductive Sciences*, 1921 (his thesis for promotion to the rank of dozent); *The Main Trends of Philosophy*, an anthology of extracts from the works of its classical representatives, 1923; *The Main Principles of Scientific Method and Formal Logic*, 1928; *The Logical Foundations of Teaching*, 1934; *Propaedeutic to Philosophy* (for colleges of general education), 1938; the present work, 1949; *Outline of Logic*, 1953 (translated into German as *Abriss der Logik*, 1958); and, posthumously, *Pragmatic Logic*, 1965.

## Ajdukiewicz's philosophy

Ajdukiewicz's first original works of importance in philosophy appeared in the 1930s and fell within the field of logic or theory of meaning. He brought to the problems of this field an understanding of the nature of deductive systems obtained from earlier work in the domain of metalogic. From the beginning he was quite clear in his mind as to the distinction between sense and reference. This had been classically articulated by Frege but had been to some extent obscured in English-speaking philosophy by the influence of Russell's theory of names, with its thesis that a true, 'logically proper' name is meaningless if it stands for nothing.

At the time Ajdukiewicz was writing, the prevailing assumption among analytic philosophers in western Europe was that meaning is essentially syntactical in character, which is to say, very approximately, that all questions about meaning can be answered by assertions about the properties of expressions or the relations of expressions to one another and need involve no statements about the relations between expressions and extralinguistic reality. The most elaborately developed version of this doctrine is Carnap's *Logical Syntax of Language*. One source of this conviction was, no doubt, Wittgenstein's view that statements about the relationship between language and the world are senseless, endeavouring to say what can only be 'shown', a view that did not prevent him from making many statements of this avowedly unacceptable kind in his *Tractatus*. Another source could have been disquiet about the concept of truth, engendered by the paradoxes to which its use seemed to give rise. Philosophers of the Vienna Circle were led by this to accepting a form of the coherence theory of truth, which saw it as a matter of the relations of sentences to one another and not to extralinguistic reality.

Ajdukiewicz rejected this point of view in his theory of meaning. In conformity to his thorough commitment to Frege's distinction between sense and reference, he thought of meanings, not as any sort of objects, but as a property of expressions determined by the existence of rules governing their employment. He distinguished three kinds of rules: (i) axiomatic rules, laying it down that certain sentences should always be accepted, for example 'every $A$ is $A$'; (ii) deductive rules, laying it down that if one sentence is accepted, another sentence must also be accepted, for example, if 'if $p$ then $q$' is accepted so also must be 'if not-$q$ then not-$p$'; and (iii) empirical rules, laying down that certain sentences must be accepted in the face of certain specified data of experience, for example 'it hurts' when one is in pain. The non-syntactical aspect of meaning, of course, is covered by the third, empirical, type of rule. Only the first two types of rule are found in formal deductive systems. The main lines of this theory were published in 1934, a year after Tarski had published in Polish his famous essay on the concept of truth which, as it were, logically legitimated semantic assertions about the relations between words and the world. In due course Carnap was converted to this point of view.

Two further fields of investigation should be briefly mentioned. On the basis of some ideas of Lesniewski's, Ajdukiewicz developed a theory of semantic categories to make possible the formulation of rules specifying which combinations of expressions are admissible as well-formed sentences. This is a simple enough task as regards an artificial, formal language of limited and specified vocabulary. It is an altogether more difficult problem as regards natural languages. To English-speaking philosophers the problem for natural languages seemed to allow for no more definite and explicit a solution than Ryle's very informal and unsystematic doctrine of categories. More recently, however, the type of procedure Ajdukiewicz inaugurated has been carried further in the kind of analysis of syntactical structure practised by Chomsky and his associates.

Ajdukiewicz went on to derive from his account of the meaning of expressions as being defined by rules which, it seemed, allowed for considerable freedom of choice, the conclusion that there could be languages which differed, not just in the comparatively trivial sense of having different vocabularies, each associated with a single common pattern of rules, but in being radically untranslatable into each other. Here he anticipated the conclusions about the indeterminacy of translation which are fundamental to Quine's work in the philosophy of language, although he arrived at them from a very different direction. He went on to infer that the epistemologist, since inevitably confined to the conceptual apparatus of the language in which his reasonings are expressed, cannot set himself up as an impartial critic of or arbiter between different conceptual apparatuses.

On his return to philosophy after 1945 Ajdukiewicz was

led to abandon the kind of conventionalism or linguistic relativism that has just been outlined, but he entertained the possibility of another doctrine familiar from the writings of Quine which takes the logical aspects of language, in Ajdukiewicz the sentences determined as acceptable by its axiomatic and deductive rules, to be as much accessible to the arbitrament of experience as are sentences of a straightforwardly empirical character. Like Quine he maintained that empirical testing bears not on single assertions, but on whole bodies of assertions, among which the propositions of logic may be included. Among other subjects treated by him in this phase of his career are definition, hypothetical statements, analyticity and, in a rare departure from strict philosophical abstraction, the freedom of science.

Fuller accounts of Ajdukiewicz's original contributions to philosophy can be found in chapter 5 of H. Skolimowski's *Polish Analytical Philosophy* and in the article about him by Z. A. Jordan in *The Encyclopedia of Philosophy*, edited by Paul Edwards.

## This book

The present volume, which was first published in 1949 at the time when the official repression of the logically oriented philosophy of Poland was just getting under way, was, it appears, one for which Ajdukiewicz had a particular affection. He may well have felt that in it he had succeeded in conveying a great deal of information about historically influential philosophical arguments without any departure from the well-established standards of clarity and rigour characteristic of the school of philosophers to which he belonged.

As a first introduction to philosophy it can withstand comparison with a much better-known work with the same aims and of much the same size: Bertrand Russell's *Problems of Philosophy*. Ajdukiewicz's book is much more neutral and

impersonal than Russell's, it is altogether drier and less enter-
taining, it contains no significant new additions to philosophical thought. On the other hand it covers more ground
and does so in a more conclusive and authoritative way.
Ajdukiewicz, with the characteristic logical self-conscious-
ness of the Polish philosophers, always has a clear idea of
what he has established and what he has not. There are no
suggestive or tentative loose ends in this book.

His conception of the scope of epistemology and metaphysics is not one that will appear at all surprising to those
brought up in the modern philosophical tradition of the
English-speaking world. There is more awareness of the
work of Husserl and the phenomenological movement than
such a book by a British or American writer would be likely
to reveal. This is expressed in particular in the use of some
of those ideas to provide more persuasive support than
Kant gave to his thesis that the propositions of mathematics, although *a priori,* are nevertheless synthetic. In
general there is a certain almost military austerity about the
conscientiousness and punctilio with which Ajdukiewicz sets
out his reasonings, as compared with the measure of genial
perfunctoriness to be found in Russell's popular philosophical
expositions. The claims of beauty take a distinctly second
place to those of truth.

The publication of this book will not make Ajdukiewicz's
own positive contributions to philosophy available to readers
of philosophy in the English-speaking world, in the way that
the publication of an English version of Kotarbinski's
*Gnosiology* made accessible his systematic body of philosophical opinions. For that we must wait for the publication in
English of a selection of his essays. But it does provide an
excellent example of the typical Polish style of philosophical
reasoning, applied to the task of introductory philosophical
exposition, in which its clarity and rigour can be as valuable
as in the domain of more advanced and original work.

## Further reading

Z. A. Jordan     *The Development of Mathematical Logic and of Logical Positivism in Poland between the two wars* (O.U.P., London, 1945)

Z. A. Jordan     *Philosophy and Ideology* (D. Reidel, Dordrecht, Holland, 1963)

H. Skolimowski *Polish Analytical Philosophy* (Routledge, London, 1967)

# *Preface*

In this short book the reader will find a review of the most important problems which are traditionally included in the theory of knowledge and metaphysics. The reader will also find a review of the solutions to these problems which are most frequently found in the history of philosophy and, in consequence, a review of philosophical tendencies and trends in the theory of knowledge and metaphysics. Alongside bare presentations of theses characteristic of various trends, that is to say alongside philosophical positions, we have in most cases sketched the course of thought which led to these positions and we have in some cases sketched the polemics which representatives of opposing schools have conducted.

When I started writing I did not intend to write an entire book. The origin of this book is as follows; twenty-five years ago I published a book of philosophical readings under the title *Main Trends of Philosophy* which I introduced with a preface containing a review of problems and trends of philosophy which were then illustrated by texts from various authors. Recently, preparing a new edition of the above mentioned readings, I came to the conclusion that the preface should be written anew. Consequently I started to write this preface again. The new version grew to such a size that it could not be contained in the same volume as the readings. The thought occurred to me of publishing the preface as a separate book. This is the origin of the volume which the reader now has in his hands.

The origin of this book explains its character. First of all it is not a textbook for advanced students in which the author writes with the greatest precision he is capable of, ignoring the requirements of easy intelligibility. On the contrary, writing this book I have avoided too far-reaching analyses and I have not attempted to achieve the sort of complete conceptual clarity which could be achieved only at the expense of intelligibility. Consequently there are some statements whose sense may not be sufficiently precise for those whose demands in this respect are very high but that will not disturb the average reader. I mention this in order to avoid the misunderstanding that I regard the formulations contained in this book as final and incapable of being rendered more precise.

However, this little book is not ideal as a first introduction to philosophy. For that purpose it is too concisely written and not all means possible for a suggestive presentation of problems and their solutions are employed here. The most suitable introduction to philosophical problems is always monographs elaborating particular problems in detail. I think, however, that this book, in conjunction with *Philosophical Readings*, which is shortly to appear, will be able to serve as such a 'first introduction'.

This book will serve best at an intermediate level. It will be able to serve as a textbook or repetitorium for those who have already acquired some philosophical knowledge before reading it. It will enable these readers to find more or less tangible formulations of trends and problems of philosophy. Perhaps it will also give some readers a chance to arrive at their own opinions about various philosophical issues.

I hope that in spite of all the shortcomings I have mentioned

*Problems and Theories* will fill a serious gap in our philosophical literature. For that literature contains hardly any books which cover the whole of theory of knowledge and metaphysics systematically. This role was once filled by 'introductions to philosophy' written by German authors at the turn of the century and now entirely out of print. These 'introductions' left too much to be desired in respect of their analysis of the meaning of philosophers' assertions. This work, in spite of compromises resulting from its level of presentation and the limits of its size, attempts to explain the meaning of terms used by philosophers in putting forward their doctrines. On this account I trust that the reader will find it useful.

July 1948                                                    K.A.

*Introduction*

# Theory of knowledge, metaphysics and other philosophical disciplines

What is philosophy? This question can be easily asked but is rather difficult to answer. The word 'philosophy' has a very long history and in different periods it has referred to different things. Never as a matter of fact has the word 'philosophy' been given a meaning precise enough for it to be used unequivocally, a meaning on which most people living at a given time would agree.

The term 'philosophy' originated in ancient Greece. Etymologically we can distinguish two components in it: *fileo* = I love, I strive, and *sophia* = wisdom, knowledge. Originally, then, the term philosophy meant for the Greeks 'love of wisdom' or 'striving for knowledge'. According to its original meaning all scientific researchers were called philosophers. Thus originally the term 'philosophy' meant the same as the term 'science'. In the course of time when as the result of the growth of knowledge it came to be beyond the capacity of a single person to master the entire scope of knowledge, specialisation of the sciences started. From the once common core, the universal science called philosophy, various sciences began to detach themselves. They acquired separate names and were no longer confused under the teaching of philosophy. From the common core of the universal science, particular specialisations detached themselves which historically originated and developed later, natural science, mathematics, history, etc. Within the original core there remained inquiries which retained the name 'philosophy' and were either cultivated on a large scale at the dawn of European thought, that is before specialisation began, or which originated later but were connected with these initial inquiries.

Until recently the name 'philosophy' covered the following disciplines: metaphysics, theory of knowledge, logic, psychology, ethics, aesthetics. At the present time, as specialisation continues further, disciplines are detaching themselves from philosophy in the last sense mentioned. Contemporary psychology, feeling closer to biology or sociology than to the other philosophical disciplines, is attempting to break away from philosophy. Contemporary logic, which in some of its parts considers itself more closely related to mathematics than to its other philosophical companions, is also breaking away. Ethics, too, if we take it to be a science of morality, not a doctrine concerning a given morality, and also aesthetics, show centrifugal tendencies. The only disciplines which are faithful to the original conception of philosophy are metaphysics, the theory of knowledge, and normative ethics, attempting to teach what is good and what is evil. To the first two of these, the most fundamental philosophical disciplines, the chapters of this book are devoted. In the chapters that follow we shall become acquainted with the rich content of these disciplines.

# Part I

# The theory of knowledge

# 1

## Classical problems of the theory of knowledge

The theory of knowledge, which is also called epistemology (from the Greek *episteme*, synonymous with the English word 'knowledge') or gnoselogy (from Greek *gnosis*, synonymous with the English word 'cognition') is – as the name shows – the science of cognition. But – what is cognition? By cognition we mean both cognitive acts and cognitive results. Cognitive acts are certain mental activities such as perception, remembering, judging, and, further, such as reasoning, reflecting, inferring and so on. Scientific assertions can serve as an example of cognitive results. Scientific assertions are not mental activities, so they are not to be included among cognitive acts. The law of gravity or the Pythagorean theorem are not mental phenomena of any kind but are the meaning of the statements in which these laws are formulated.

Does the theory of knowledge, which we said was the science of cognition, concern itself with cognitive acts or cognitive results? If we answer this question by examining what has actually taken place in the history of the theory of knowledge, we have to reply that both cognitive acts and cognitive results have been the subject of investigation.

If the theory of knowledge occupies itself with cognitive acts, that is with certain mental phenomena, it is then concerned with the same things as psychology in one of its parts. Psychology in fact deals with mental phenomena and consequently with cognitive acts. But although psychology and the theory of knowledge overlap to some extent, nevertheless each of these disciplines investigates the subject-matter from its own point of view. Psychology is concerned with the actual occurrence of cognitive processes. It attempts to describe and classify them and to find laws covering their occurrence. The theory of knowledge is concerned with something quite different.

Cognitive acts and results are the subjects of evaluation. They are evaluated from the point of view of their truth or falsity; we evaluate them also from the point of view of their justification. Now the actual occurrence of cognitive processes, which is the business of psychology, is of no interest to the theory of knowledge, which is interested, however, in the standards by which cognition is evaluated and thus in truth and falsity, justification or baselessness. What is truth? This is the first of the fundamental questions of the theory of knowledge, the problem of the essence of truth. The second classical problem of the theory of knowledge is the problem of the sources of cognition. In this problem we are concerned with what, in the last analysis, cognition should be based on and with the methods for arriving at it, if it is to be fully justified cognition of reality. The third classical problem of the theory of knowledge is the problem of the limits of cognition; it calls for an answer to the question what can be the subject of cognition and in particular, whether a reality which is independent of the subject of cognition can be cognised (known). We shall be satisfied for the time being with these general formulations of the three classical problems of the theory of knowledge and we shall go on to examine the solutions that have been given to them.

# 2

## The problem of truth

### The classical definition of truth and objections to it

What is truth? The classical answer to this question states that the truth of a thought consists in its agreement with reality. *Veritas est adaequatio rei et intellectus*: this was the classical answer in its scholastic formulation. But what is this agreement of thought and reality, as the basis of the definition of truth? Certainly not that the thought itself is identical with the reality it describes. Perhaps then in this, that this thought is a likeness of something real, is a reflection of a reality. But even this interpretation of the 'agreement of thought with reality' seems to some philosophers an absurd idea. How, they ask, could thought be a likeness of something quite different from it, how can thought which is something that has time-dimensions but no others, be a likeness of something that is spatial, how can thought resemble a cube or Niagara Falls? Furthermore, even regarding the time-duration itself, a thought in order to be true does not have to be like the reality it is concerned with. In order to be true a thought concerned with a short-lasting phenomenon does not have to be short-lasting. Thus a thought may fail to resemble reality and nevertheless be a true thought.

The defenders of the classical definition of truth reply to

such criticisms by pointing out that the process which is the act of thought is one thing and its content another. They emphasise that it is not the process of thinking itself which ought to resemble reality but the content of the thought must resemble it if it is to be true. But even this does not satisfy the critics of the classical definition of truth. They point out that the concept of likeness is by no means a clear one. Likeness consists in a partial identity of characteristics; what part of their characteristics must be common to two objects for them to be called alike? This is by no means clearly determined. Consequently the definition describing as true those thoughts whose content resembles something real would be an imprecise definition, since it would not determine how far the likeness between the content of the thought and reality must extend for the thought to be true. Since this agreement of thought with reality does not amount to either identity or likeness between the two, the question is – say the critics of the classical definition of truth – what does this agreement finally consist in? Unable to find a satisfactory answer to this question, the opponents of the classical definition of truth come to the conclusion that this definition is devoid of genuine content.

But there is another line of thought which leads some thinkers to the rejection of the classical definition of truth. Some philosophers reject it and look for another definition because they think that it cannot be determined at all whether our thoughts agree with reality. If truth consists in agreement of thought with reality then we could not know of anything whether it was true or false. The conception of truth as agreement of thought with reality should, therefore, be given up as an unattainable ideal and should be replaced by another concept of truth which would enable us to determine whether our thoughts and assertions are true or not.

The opinion that we cannot ascertain the agreement of thought with reality is based on the arguments of ancient sceptics which could be summarised as follows: if someone wants to know whether a given thought or assertion agrees with reality then he would have to know for this purpose not only the thought itself but he would have to know reality as well. How can he do this? He will refer to experience, he will reason in this way or another, in short he will apply certain methods or criteria. But where is the certainty that cognition obtained by means of these criteria reveals undistorted reality to us? For this reason we should have to inspect our criteria. This inspection is carried out by applying the same or perhaps different criteria. In one way or another the validity of this inspection will depend on the validity of the criteria used in it and this again is doubtful and requires further investigation; in this investigation once again some criteria will be applied, and so on ad infinitum. In a word, we shall never be able to have justified knowledge of reality and because of this we shall never be able to know whether our thoughts agree with reality or not.

## Truth as agreement with criteria

The line of thought sketched above has led many philosophers to reject the definition of truth as agreement of thought with reality and to replace it with another definition of truth. This new definition of truth is arrived at in roughly the following way: let us consider the way in which we actually use the term 'truth'. In this way we shall perhaps be better able to become aware what this term really means for us. Undoubtedly everyone is ready to acknowledge as true an assertion in which he believes himself, which corresponds to his convictions. If one believes that $A$ is $B$ one is ready to assert a statement affirming that $A$ is $B$ is true, and conversely. If one attributes truth to an assertion, one is ready to believe what it asserts. However, no-one will contend that a true assertion is the same thing as an assertion one believes in.

Everyone is aware that there are true assertions in which he does not believe if only because he does not know them. On the other hand, no-one considers himself infallible and everyone knows that there are assertions which he believes but are not true. We are fully aware that not all our convictions have been gained by means of scrupulous and systematic inquiries but that we arrived at them by applying methods, that is to say criteria, whose validity must be questioned and which must be replaced when confronted with more authoritative criteria. Only if we had arrived at our convictions by applying criteria which are final and irrevocable and from which there is no appeal would we unhesitatingly recognise all these convictions as true ones.

These and similar lines of argument suggest to some philosophers the following definition of truth: *a true assertion is the same thing as an assertion which satisfies final and irrevocable criteria*. There is no other way of becoming convinced about the truth of an assertion than by testing it with the final criterion whose verdict is irrevocable, in the sense that the verdict of any other criterion must give way to it. Whether an assertion which passes the test of this final criterion does or does not agree with reality we cannot know and – as the sceptics have shown – we shall never be able to know. Consequently when distinguishing truth from falsity the point is not whether a given assertion agrees with reality or not but whether it agrees with the final criteria. Thus in order to define the concept of truth according to our actual use of this notion we should define truth as *agreement of thought with final and irrevocable criteria*.

## Nonclassical definitions of truth

This conception of truth is given different forms by its different adherents in accordance with whatever is considered to be the final criterion.

Thus, for example, the *coherence theory of truth* defines truth as agreement of thoughts among themselves. The adherents of this theory consider that the final and irrevocable criterion which determines whether a given assertion is to be accepted or rejected is its agreement with other assertions accepted already; the agreement consists in this, that a given assertion does not contradict the others and harmonise with the rest of the system. It might appear that the verdict of experience is the final criterion but this is not the case because, above the verdict of experience, there is a higher court which is the criterion of agreement. Let us consider a teaspoon submerged in a glass of water. The verdict of sight tells us that the spoon is bent, the verdict of touch that it is straight. Why do we believe touch here and not sight? Because the assertion supported by sight does not harmonise with the rest of our knowledge (for example, the way in which the seemingly unsupported upper part of the spoon stands out of the water contradicts the law of falling bodies): on the other hand, the assertion supported by touch (that the spoon is continuous) agrees perfectly with the rest of our knowledge It is just the agreement of this assertion with all other accepted assertions and not the verdict of the senses alone (which in this case leads to a contradiction) which is the final court irrevocably determining its acceptance.

It has been argued against the adherents of the coherence theory of truth that the agreement of thoughts among themselves cannot be the sufficient criterion of truth. If it were then every consistent and coherent story could be considered as true just as much as a physical theory based on laborious observations and experiments. Coherentists could defend their position by making their conception moe precise. They are concerned with the agreement of a given thought not with any set of thoughts whatever but with its agreement with assertions supported by experience. But, even here, out of the body of assertions supported by experience not one but many harmonious systems of harmonious assertions can be constructed. Choosing one system we shall have to consider as falsehood, as an illusion, some assertions based on experience which in another system will have to be considered true because they harmonise with it. Agreement with experience alone and internal harmony are thus not sufficient. There must be another, additional criterion that would enable us to choose among various systems of consistent assertions which agree with reality. In actual fact this additional criterion of choice between coherent systems has been provided, in more developed versions of the coherence theory of truth. For example, simplicity of the system, economy of means etc, have been suggested as this additional criterion. These considerations are undoubtedly valuable as an attempt to become aware of what our guide-lines are in accepting assertions of natural science independently of the doubtful coherentist definition of truth.

A further line adopted by some adherents of the coherence conception of truth is worth mentioning. If the truth of an assertion is to be decided by its agreement with assertions based on experience, then the question arises whether we mean here the agreement with the assertions supported by experience hitherto or whether we mean agreement with both experience hitherto and future experience. If the latter is the case we cannot decide today, when future experience is unknown, whether any assertion is true or not. An assertion can harmonise perfectly with assertions hitherto accepted but we cannot predict whether future experience will not force us to reconstruct our system in such a way that a given assertion will clash with it. If truth were to consist in agreement of an assertion with the whole system embracing both present and future experience then only at infinity can we know whether a given assertion is true or not. Developing such ideas some philosophers (for example, neo-Kantians of the Marburg school) arrived at the following formulation:

truth is an infinite process. For the adherents of this position (and there are many besides neo-Kantians) there is really no final and irrevocable criterion and because of this there are no assertions which could be finally accepted and which could not be rejected (for example, as the result of new data of experience). All assertions are revocable, both assertions functioning as hypotheses and theories as well as assertions directly based on experience. Nothing can be asserted finally and irrevocably; every assertion is tentative.

Others again attempt to find the final and irrevocable criterion determining the acceptance of a given assertion in *universal agreement*. If I hear in the stillness of the night a soft continuous whirring noise and I want to know whether this noise really exists or whether I am the victim of a subjective illusion, I ask the other people who are with me whether they hear the noise. If the others hear it too, I believe the verdict of my ears. These and similar considerations induce some to see the final and irrevocable criterion in universal agreement. Since truth is to consist in agreement with this criterion, then the definition suggests itself according to which the truth of a given assertion consists in universal agreement about it. This concept of 'universal agreement' requires further elucidation; we do not mean that a given assertion is to be accepted only when everyone living, dead and yet to be born agrees about it. Depending on the way in which this 'universal agreement' is defined, the concept of truth discussed here takes different forms.

Others yet again see in *self-evidence* this final criterion irrevocably decisive for the acceptance of a given assertion. This self-evidence not only makes a given assertion indubitable to us but furthermore it assures us that everybody who understands it will have to accept it. The adherents of this conception attempt to analyse what this 'self-evidence' consists in: sometimes they reduce it to the 'clear and distinct' presentation of the state of affairs with which a given assertion is concerned (Descartes), sometimes a different interpretation is given. Thus, for example, the representative of the Baden school of neo-Kantians, the German philosopher Rickert, points out that when an assertion seems self-evident to us then it is forced upon us with necessity which we feel as an obligation. A given assertion is self-evident when we feel we ought to accept it. But every duty, every obligation, corresponds to a prescription containing a command, that is to say a norm. Self-evident assertions therefore point to a certain norm governing the acceptance of assertions. This norm is independent of us, lies beyond us, and because of this Rickert calls it the transcendental norm. Thus a self-evident assertion is the same as an assertion in agreement with the transcendental norm.

The opponents of the classical definition of truth for whom truth consists in the agreement of thought with final criteria and who see this final criterion in self-evidence come to the conclusion that the truth of a thought consists in its self-evidence, understood in one way or another. For Rickert, for example, the truth of a given thought consists in its agreement with the transcendental norm.

Another well-known conception of truth is developed by *pragmatism*. This is not a homogeneous doctrine and its adherents define truth in various different ways. In its radical form pragmatism contends, as a point of departure, that the truth of a given assertion consists in its agreement with final criteria. However, these final criteria are considered by pragmatism, in its radical form, to be the utility of a given assertion for action. Hence the definition *identifying the truth of a given assertion with its utility*. The pragmatist argument is roughly as follows: our intellectual functions, and thus for example our convictions, are not independent of our practical activity. Our convictions influence our action, give it a direction, point out to the agent means leading to his intended aim. If this influence of our convictions on our action makes the action effective, that is enables us to achieve our intended aims, then the conviction is true. Entering a dark room, for example, I wish to switch on the light. I conjecture that the switch is to the right of the door. This conviction of mine (together with my desire to switch on the light) directs my hand to the right of the door, so it gives a specific direction to my action. If the action directed in this way by my conviction leads to the desired switching on of the light, it was true. If on the other hand the action leading in the direction determined by my conviction turns out to be unsuccessful, then my conviction was false. As I have already said, the identification of truth with utility is characteristic of only the radical version of pragmatism. In its less radical versions pragmatism does not go so far but in its main tendency gravitates towards empiricism and positivism, which we shall now discuss.

## A proper formulation of the classical concept of truth

We have given above a short and by no means exhaustive review of various conceptions of truth, distinct from the classical one. All of them see the essence of truth in the agreement of thought with criteria, that is methods which finally decide whether a given assertion is to be accepted or rejected. Inquiries devoted to the discovery of these highest criteria of our judgement are sometimes interesting and instructive but to see the essence of truth in the agreement of thought with these criteria is a false concept of truth. The content of this concept is better expressed by the classical definition according to which a true thought is a thought which agrees with reality. At the beginning of this chapter some objections were stated to this definition, pointing out that it is not clear what this agreement of thought with reality consists in. However, an attempt to grasp the essence of this agreement is not as hopeless as it is made out to be by the critics of the classical definition of truth. If a given assertion agrees with reality it means that the state of affairs is as the assertion describes it. So the thought that the earth is round agrees with reality because the earth is round; the thought that the sun is bigger than the earth agrees with reality because the sun really is bigger than the earth. Consequently the basic idea of the classical definition of truth could be expressed in the following way: thought $T$ is true – this means: thought $T$ asserts that such-and-such is the case and such-and-such really is the case. With this last formulation of the classical definition of truth some difficulties of a logical nature are connected which require some caution in the use of this definition. We shall not analyse this matter here, however.

Against such a formulation of the classical definition of truth the sceptic's objection is no longer dangerous. That objection says that we can never know whether the thought that the earth is round agrees with reality, but to know that is the same as to know that the earth is round, as we have said that for a given assertion to agree with reality means simply that what is said to be the case is the case. If the sceptic asserts that we cannot know whether the thought that the earth is round agrees with reality, then he asserts thereby that we cannot know that the earth is round. Generally, when the sceptics assert that we can never know whether a thought agrees with reality, then from this assertion it follows that we can never know about anything. Because in order to know something we would have to know that the thought which asserts this fact agrees with reality.

## Scepticism and its refutation

The sceptics have gone so far as to assert that we can know nothing, that is to say that we have no justifiable knowledge about anything. In order to possess such knowledge, the sceptics argued, we should have to justify it by applying a method, that is by following a certain criterion. However, the knowledge obtained in accordance with this criterion would be justified only if we knew beforehand that the criterion applied by us is a trustworthy one, is a criterion which always leads to truth and never to falsehood. In order to know whether our criterion is a trustworthy one we should have to apply another criterion which again would have to be examined critically before we could trust it, etc. *ad infinitum*. It is not possible, then, to find a way which would lead us to justifiable knowledge about anything.

Someone who was convinced by the sceptics would have to accept that on no subject can we gain justifiable knowledge, that such and such is the case, consequently we could not assert that any thought is justified, that it agrees with reality. If the sceptics' reasoning were accepted, we should have to agree that we can never gain justifiable knowledge about the fact that a given thought is true, understanding the word 'true' according to the classical definition.

The difficulties brought forward by the sceptics are directed not only at the classical definition but they affect equally strongly the nonclassical definitions which describe truth of a thought as agreement with criteria. If it is the case – as the sceptics argue – that we cannot gain justifiable knowledge about anything, then we cannot gain this knowledge about the fact of agreement between thoughts and criteria. There is no reason then which would compel us in trying to avoid difficulties arising from the sceptics' arguments against the classical definition of truth to accept the definition identifying the truth of a thought with agreement with criteria instead. By giving up the classical definition and accepting another we are exposed in equal measure to the objection that truth defined in one way or another is unknowable.

Is it the case, however, that the sceptics' reasoning justifies this desperate thesis? If we answer this question in the affirmative and acknowledge the sceptics' reasoning as valid, we should by accepting the sceptics' thesis involve ourselves in a contradiction. On the one hand, by accepting the sceptics' thesis we should assert that nothing can be justified; on the other hand, however, by accepting that the sceptics' reasoning justifies their thesis, we should admit, against the sceptics' thesis, that something can be justified (namely at least the sceptics' thesis itself). The sceptics themselves were aware of this difficulty. In order to avoid it they pointed out that their thesis about the impossibility of justified knowledge is not asserted categorically but that they only confess that that is how it seems to them while they themselves suspend judgement as to whether it is really the case. The sceptics did not feel entitled to any opinion beyond the awareness of what takes place in their minds, beyond therefore what they feel, think, etc. They described themselves as those who search for the truth but who so far have not found it (hence their name, because *skeptomai* in Greek means 'I search, look around').

Disregarding the difficulties of the sceptical position just discussed, we can easily see a mistake that is contained in the sceptics' reasoning. The sceptics assert that in order to gain justified knowledge it must be arrived at by applying a criterion about which we should know beforehand that it is trustworthy. In other words, in order to gain justified knowledge of any kind we have to have at our disposal according to the sceptics not only a trustworthy criterion by means of which we would justify this knowledge but furthermore would have to know that this criterion itself is trustworthy. It is just here that the sceptics' mistake is to be found. The point is that in order to justify an assertion it is sufficient to arrive at it by applying a trustworthy criterion and we do not have to know also that the criterion applied is trustworthy. The knowledge of whether our criterion is trustworthy is not necessary for the justification of the assertion arrived at in accordance with it. It is required only to assure us that we have justified a given assertion. It is one thing to justify an assertion and another to know that one has done so. It is one thing to do something well and it is another to know that one has done so. Thus if the knowledge that the criterion applied in the justification of an assertion is trustworthy is not necessary for the justification of this assertion, then the premise is false from which the sceptics drew their conclusion that the justification of any assertion whatsoever requires an infinite number of steps of reasoning which can never be completed (it is false that it leads to a *regressus ad infinitum*).

## Nonclassical definitions of truth as leading to idealism

We have seen that the reasons for which some philosophers rejected the classical definition of truth were: first, improper formulations of the basic idea of what is involved in the classical concept of truth; secondly, the critical opinion of the sceptics about the possibilty of knowledge of reality. After having found a correct formulation for the classical concept of truth and after having parried the objections of the sceptics, we have come to the conclusion, however, that there is no reason for giving up the classical definition and choosing another nonclassical one. These nonclassical definitions of truth have played an important role in the history of philosophical thought; they became one of the points of departure for idealism according to which the world accessible to cognition is not taken to be the true reality; that world is reduced to the role of a construction of thought and thus to a kind of fiction different from poetic fiction only in being constructed according to some regular criteria on which we finally rely in making judgements.

# 3

## Problems of the source of knowledge

### Psychological and epistemological versions of this problem

Initially the problem of the source of knowledge was taken to be psychological inquiries concerning the factual genesis of our concepts, judgements and thoughts in general. There was controversy as to whether among the concepts which we came across in the mind of an adult human being there are innate thoughts and concepts, or whether the concepts and thoughts which we possess are entirely formed by experience. *Those who believe in the existence of innate ideas are called genetical rationalists or nativists; those who hold the opposite opinion are called genetical empiricists.* According to the nativists some of our ideas and beliefs are innate in the sense that our minds are so constructed that they must arrive at these and no other ideas, at these and no other beliefs, independently of what is provided to them by the senses and introspection. The senses do not, according to the nativists, have any influence on the content of some at least of our ideas and beliefs. The role of the senses is confined to that of liberating certain ideas potentially contained in the organisation of the human mind. Among adherents of this view were Plato, Descartes and Leibniz.

The adherents of genetic empiricism claimed, contrary to

the nativists, that the human mind is a blank tablet (*tabula rasa*) on which experience writes its signs. Initially these signs are impressions, from them derive their reproductions in memory, derivative representations whose various combinations and elaborations lead to more or less complex ideas; these elaborations are sometimes so intricate that it is not easy to trace the original, that is the impressions from which they ultimately derive. The genetical empiricists express this opinion in a concise formula: *nihil est in intellectu quod non prius fuerit in sensu* ('there is nothing in the mind which has not been previously in the senses'). The most representative genetical empiricists were, first of all, the British philosophers of the seventeenth and eighteenth centuries, John Locke, David Hume and others. They exerted themselves to show how, out of the material provided by impressions of the senses, our other ideas originate, particularly ideas of a high level of abstraction. The French philosopher Condillac attempted to represent this process of the development of the mind of adult human beings by means of the model of a statue, gradually endowed with different sense-organs through which ever new impressions arrive and he showed how these impressions are transformed into the higher products of the mind. Hume used the thesis of genetic empiricism to unmask certain expressions as having only a fictitious meaning. According to the empiricist thesis, every concept must show its experiential origin if it is to be recognised as valid. If we cannot show for a given expression that it somehow derives from experience then its meaning is only apparent.

Hume's arguments aroused a ferment which inspired his successors to undertake the analysis of expressions more thoroughly. In the course of time the postulate that every expression must show its experiential origin was replaced by a related postulate. In recent times we have come to recognise as significant only an expression whose meaning equips us with a method that enables us to apply it to objects, that is which enables us to decide whether these objects can or cannot be named by this word. This postulate, which is the slogan of present-day operationalism, has turned out to be very fruitful for the development of natural science. Among other things, it became the point of departure for the revolution in modern physics that was initiated by Einstein's theory of relativity. Einstein starts with the rejection of the concept of absolute simultaneity of two events and replaces it with the concept of simultaneity relative to a given spatial system and so relative to a set of bodies. Einstein rejects the concept of absolute simultaneity just because there is no method which would enable us to determine on the basis of experience whether two events separated in space are simultaneous in the absolute sense or not.

The problem of genetic rationalism and empiricism as dealing with the origin of our ideas and beliefs, which we have briefly discussed, is a problem of a distinctly psychological character. It is concerned in actual fact with the way in which thoughts come to be in the human mind. With this psychological problem there has been connected, and sometimes confused, another problem, not psychological, but methodological or epistemological in character. This is the problem of how we can arrive at fully justified knowledge of reality, that is by what methods we can arrive at knowledge which is true. This problem belongs to the theory of knowledge, that is to the discipline which is concerned, not with the factual occurrence of cognition, but with its truth and justification. To this problem we shall now turn our attention.

There are two pairs of opposed positions with regard to it. *Rationalism and empiricism* is the first pair, *rationalism and irrationalism* is the second one. In the names of these positions the terms rationalism and empiricism, which we came across in the discussion of the problem of the psychological origin of our ideas, occur again. But here they mean something quite different. Because of this in the previous discussion the terms 'rationalism' and 'empiricism' were prefaced with the word 'genetic'; now, in contrast, we should talk about methodological rationalism and empiricism. But even by doing this we have not removed all ambiguity because the term 'rationalism' (of the methodological sort) has a different meaning when it is contrasted with empiricism from what it has when contrasted with irrationalism. Because of this we shall not describe as rationalism the position opposed to methodological empiricism but we shall call it apriorism, leaving the term 'rationalism' to denote the position opposed to irrationalism. In the cases where the misunderstanding might occur all the same we shall call this rationalism *anti-irrationalism*.

After all these introductory remarks we shall first discuss the dispute between *methodological apriorism and empiricism* and then discuss the core of the dispute between *rationalism* (anti-irrationalism) and *irrationalism*.


## Apriorism and empiricism

We shall begin with apriorism and empiricism. This dispute is concerned with the evaluation of the role which experience plays in our cognition, that is, what the role of our senses and introspection is in perception. The perceptions which we owe to the senses inform us about objects and events in the external world (the physical world) and consist of external experience; the perceptions which we owe to introspection inform us about our own mental states (for example, about the fact that I am sad or joyful) and they consist of internal experience. Now empiricism of all varieties attributes to experience the dominant role in our cognition, apriorism on the other hand emphasises the role of apriori cognition, that is cognition independent of experience.

## Radical apriorism

The dispute between empiricism and apriorism has taken various forms in the history of philosophy. At the dawn of European philosophical thought in ancient Greece apriorism was in the ascendant and it denied that experience was of any value for the cognition of reality; it judged knowledge based on experience to be merely apparent, to be something that merely acquaints us with the appearance of reality and not with genuine reality. The point of departure for this depreciation of the value of cognition based on experience was the illusions of the senses which undermine our confidence in the verdict of experience. Furthermore, there was lack of confidence in this verdict resulting from the discovery of subjective differences in the perception of various people concerned with the same object. The main reason, however, that induced some ancient philosophers to deny any credit to experience was the conviction that what is genuinely real must be unchangeable. They argued that what changes contains a contradiction because it is of a certain kind, at one time, and is not of that kind, at a later time. (They constructed various other subtle proofs that all change implies contradiction.) However, according to their opinion, whatever is contradictory in itself cannot exist. Because experience reveals to us objects which are changeable, what it presents to us is not a genuine reality but only its appearance. According to the ancient apriorists only thought, independent of all experience, that is reason, can give us acquaintance with reality.

The assertion *that only reason and not experience acquaints us with reality was the thesis of radical apriorism.* This trend had its adherents almost entirely among ancient thinkers. It had a detrimental influence on the development of the sciences because it diverted men's minds from empirical investigation, and often directed them towards fruitless speculations. It thus delayed the process of scientific cognition of nature, that is the natural sciences. It also prepared the ground for the point of view which belittles the significance of earthly life and demands that real values be sought for beyond it. From the time when the requirements of practical life appeared to be a strong enough motive to break through this prejudice against the empirical investigation of nature, from the time when empirical investigations in modern natural science began to flourish in the post-renaissance era, radical apriorism almost ceased to exist.

In more recent times the controversy between apriorism, which calls for the recognition of the cognitive value of facts independent of experience (aprioristic), and empiricism, which emphasises the significance of experience, has taken on a different character. The dispute is no longer about whether experience or reason acquaints us with genuine reality but rather whether we have any right at all to accept an assertion which is not based on experience, directly or indirectly. Assertions which we have a right to accept but which are not based on experience are called *a priori* assertions.

## Radical empiricism

Radical empiricism asserts that any justified assertion must be based on experience, directly or indirectly. Even the axioms of mathematics, even the first principles of logic, which appear to be least of all connected to experience, are, according to radical empiricism, empirical assertions (that is, based on experience). They are, according to this school of thought, nothing but inductive generalisations based on singular assertions with which experience has acquainted us.

## Moderate empiricism

This radical empiricism is opposed both by moderate

27

apriorism and moderate empiricism. Both these trends hold that there are assertions which are legitimate in science but which are nevertheless not based on experience, that is are *a priori* assertions. The difference between moderate empiricism and moderate apriorism is that they attach different significances to the role of these legitimate assertions. Moderate empiricism recognises as legitimate only such aprioristic assertions as merely explicate the meaning contained in their terms. We can thus assert *a priori* that every square has four sides, that all radii of a circle are equal to each other, etc. In order to assert this we do not have to have recourse to experience; it is enough to know what the term 'square' or 'circle' means. We need not fear that any experience could contradict such assertions, that is, for example, that experience could force us to accept that not every square has four sides. In order to do this, experience would have to present something to us which would be called a 'square' and to which nevertheless we would deny the possession of four sides. However, the very meaning of the word 'square' (the very content of the concept 'square') is such that anybody who assigned the name 'square' to a figure which he knows not to have four sides would violate this meaning. It is not possible therefore to employ the term 'square' in its normal meaning and to call a figure that is other than four-sided by this name.

Now moderate empiricism considers as legitimate *a priori* assertions only those which, as illustrated by the above example, do no more than explicate the meaning of the terms contained in them. Such assertions can be found among explicit or implicit definitions (see pp. 32–5) establishing the meanings of certain terms and among logical consequences of such definitions. Since Kant, assertions of this kind have been called *analytic* (analytic sentences, analytic judgements). So the thesis of moderate empiricism can be concisely expressed in the formula: *the only legitimate a priori assertions are analytic.*

Moderate apriorism holds on the other hand that there are legitimate *a priori* assertions which at the same time are not analytic. These assertions which are not analytic are called *synthetic* (synthetic sentences, synthetic judgements). An assertion is thus synthetic when it is not confined to the elucidation of the meaning of the terms contained in it, when it is not merely a definition, explicit or implicit, establishing the meaning of certain terms or a logical consequence of such a definition, but is a factual assertion that can be confirmed or refuted by experience. The assertion that the first emperor of the French was short is a synthetic assertion because it does not follow from the definition of the terms contained in it. On the other hand, the assertion that the first emperor of the French was a monarch is an analytic assertion, because it follows from the definition of the term 'emperor'.

The majority of synthetic assertions are undoubtedly based on experience. The disputable issue is only whether all synthetic assertions without exception must derive their justification from experience or whether there are legitimate synthetic judgements which do not derive their justification from experience, that is to say, *a priori* judgements. It is just this question which is the modern form of the problem of empiricism and apriorism. *Empiricism denies that there are legitimate synthetic judgements a priori, moderate apriorism asserts on the other hand that there are.*

In order to illustrate the way in which moderate apriorism justifies its thesis, let us take the geometrical assertion affirming that the sum of two sides of a triangle is greater than the third side. According to the apriorist this is not an analytic assertion because it does not follow from the definition of the triangle and its sides. However, according to the apriorists we can assure ourselves of the truth of this assertion without recourse to experience. It is enough to imagine a line which could serve as the base of a triangle with two lines coming from its two ends which taken together would be shorter than or equal to the base. Our imagination tells us at once that when these two lines are rotated around the base the points not adjacent to the base will never meet to form a triangle. We do not have to have recourse to experience, we do not have to rely on perception in order to assert categorically a synthetic judgement that the sum of two sides of a triangle must be greater than its third side.

The above example illustrates at the same time the way in which, according to apriorists, we arrive at synthetic *a priori* judgements. We owe them to a capacity which allows us to find general regularities in objects immediately given to us and not only to perceive individual facts, as with ordinary experience. By imagining these two sides we come to see in them a general law which claims that in *every* triangle the sum of two sides *must* be greater than the third side. The effort of our imagination thus enables us to discover a certain general regularity and not only the individual fact that in a given triangle the sum of two sides is greater than the third side, the fact for whose discovery ordinary perception would be sufficient. The capacity which enables us to discover general regularities in objects immediately given to us is called by some pure intuition (Kant), the intuition of essences (Husserl), etc.

### The dispute between empiricism and apriorism about the character of mathematical assertions

The dispute between empiricism and apriorism in its modern form is chiefly concerned with the character of mathematical assertions. *Radical empiricism considers all mathematical assertions to be based on experience.* On the other hand, *apriorism considers them to be a priori assertions* which we can accept independently of experience, to be *a priori* assertions; at the same time apriorism (we mean here moderate apriorism because it is only this form of apriorism that we find in modern times) *ascribes to at least some mathematical assertions the character of synthetic judgements. Moderate empiricism, finally, distinguishes between pure mathematics and applied mathematics and considers the assertions of pure mathematics to be a priori, ascribing to them, however, the character of analytic judgements; in applied mathematics, on the other hand, moderate empiricism recognises, in addition to certain analytic assertions, also synthetic ones,* which are considered here to be *empirical,* that is based on experience.

## Pure and applied mathematics

What is the difference between pure and applied mathematics? The difference consists in the way in which mathematical terms are understood in the two. We can perhaps best explain it with a geometrical example. In geometry there occur such terms as solid, sphere, cube, cone, etc. They also occur in ordinary language which we use in practical life when not doing mathematics. Each of these terms possesses in ordinary language an empirical sense, one that provides us with a method according to which, relying on experience (on the verdict of the senses) we can convince ourselves as to whether a given object can be called by this name or not. For example, the meaning of the word 'cube' is such that everybody who attaches this meaning to the word is able by counting the faces of a solid given to him, by measuring the angles and sides of its faces, to convince himself experientially (within the limits of error of measurement) whether a given solid is a cube or not. We are equipped with a method by which we can convince ourselves of this by the meaning with which the word 'cube' itself is endowed by ordinary language. Now in doing geometry we can take terms common to it and ordinary language in the sense that they have in ordinary language, that is in the empirical sense, the sense that enables us to decide about (at least some) statements made up of these terms on the basis of experience. If in doing geometry we ascribe an empirical sense to its terms we do it as a branch of applied mathematics.

There is, however, another way of doing the subject. In this second way we employ, as a matter of fact, the same words we use when doing geometry as a branch of applied mathematics, but we attribute a quite different meaning to them. Terms such as 'sphere' and 'cube' are deprived of the meaning that they have in ordinary language and, in particular, are deprived of any empirical sense. Once they are deprived of their original meaning we endow them with a new meaning. This is sometimes done by means of explicit definition. However, every explicit definition of a given term consists in reducing it to other terms. An explicit definition of a given term enables us to translate every sentence containing the defined term into a sentence in which this term is replaced by the other terms used in its definition. For example, the definition 'a sphere is a solid in which there is a point equidistant from all the points on its surface' enables us to translate every sentence containing the word 'sphere' into a sentence in which the word 'sphere' does not occur, but is replaced by the expression 'solid in which there is a point equidistant from all the points on its surface'.

The following question therefore arises: words such as 'sphere', 'cube', etc., are reduced by means of definition to other geometrical terms which have already been deprived of the meaning they have in ordinary language. But what sense is to be given to these terms to which we reduce the terms we are defining? Perhaps we shall reduce these terms by means of further definitions but we shall not be able to retrogress in this way to infinity and we shall have to break this chain of definitions at some terms which will serve as the point of departure for our whole system of definitions. These initial terms are called primitive terms. In what sense can these primitive terms be taken? Are they taken in the established meaning, that is the meaning these terms already possessed in ordinary language, or do we depart from the established meaning and endow them with a new meaning? Now in doing geometry as a branch of pure and not applied mathematics, primitive terms are also deprived of their established meaning and we endow them with new meanings.

But one might say these primitive terms cannot be defined because they are the point of departure of all definitions. We cannot therefore endow them with meaning but we should at least take these terms in their established meaning, that is the meaning they possess in ordinary language. This line of reasoning, however, would be mistaken. From the fact that these terms cannot be defined by means of explicit definitions, it does not follow at all that we cannot endow them with meaning. What should be done in order to endow a word with a meaning? We must establish for a certain group of people, who are going to use this word, a definitive way of understanding it. Each of us from learning his native language in early childhood has been introduced by his parents and teachers to a definitive way of understanding the words of this language. There are, however, not many words in our native language which we have come to understand by having them defined for us. There is, therefore, undoubtedly another way of introducing us to a specific way of understanding words besides definition. This way is employed when we learn a foreign language by means of what is called the direct method. When using this method the teacher does not dictate words to the pupil, that is to say does not translate words of a foreign language into the pupil's own but the teacher utters whole sentences of the foreign language. The teacher of French pointing his finger first at a table says *c'est une table*, secondly, pointing at a book says *c'est un livre*, and thirdly pointing at a pencil says *c'est un crayon*, and the pupil grasps not only that *table* means 'table', *livre* means 'book', etc., but also that the expression *c'est* corresponds to the abstract expression 'this is'. It was very much in this way that we learned adult speech when we were children. Listening to adults' utterances produced in different situations, we have acquired an ability to use these expressions in the same way and thereby we have learned how to understand these utterances as adults understand them.

The point is that we use the same method when we are doing pure mathematics, that is when we endow primitive terms with meaning, the terms which are the point of departure for all definitions. We thus utter certain statements which contain these primitive terms alongside other expressions, themselves assumed to be understood in a definitive way already. The hearer is supposed to abstract from the meaning which he previously attached to these terms but which are now treated as primitive terms and are now to obtain their sense from the statements in which they occur. We thus utter a statement 'two points determine one and only one straight line'. The hearer is supposed to forget about the meaning he previously attached to the expressions 'point' and 'straight' which are primitive terms of geometry, preserving only the established meaning of the expressions 'two' and 'determine one and only one' which do not belong among the terms specific to geometry. Once he has forgotten the established meaning of the terms 'point' and 'straight' he is supposed to understand these terms in such a way that he could believe that two points always determine one and only one straight line.

These statements which endow the primitive terms of geometry with meaning in the way described are called the axioms of this discipline. Axioms play a role similar to that played by equations with several variables. A set of equations containing two or more unknowns determines their values in a certain way. The values of the unknowns are thus those numbers which if substituted for the unknowns satisfy the equations, that is transform them into true formulae. Similarly the axioms determine the meaning of primitive terms contained in them as expressions of unknown meaning. Thus they determine the meaning we should attach to these primitive terms in order to satisfy the axioms.

Because axioms determine the meaning of the primitive terms contained in them in the way described, they are sometimes called implicit definitions, in contrast to explicit ones. Explicit definitions give the meaning of terms through equivalences, that is to say straightforwardly; axioms, on the other hand, do not provide equivalences for the terms being endowed with meaning, but they enable us to extract this meaning in much the same way as a set of equations enables us to extract the values of the unknowns contained in them.

We can therefore do geometry in abstraction from the colloquial sense of geometrical terms and endowing them with meaning with the aid of a set of implicit and explicit definitions. When we do geometry in this way we treat it as a branch of pure mathematics. The basic difference between doing pure and applied geometry consists in the fact that in applied geometry the geometrical terms possess a specific meaning independent of axioms and this is empirical meaning; because of this we can determine the truth of statements made with these terms in an empirical way. In pure geometry, on the other hand, geometrical terms do not possess any other sense but the one determined by the axioms: thus they mean what they ought to mean if the axioms are to be true and they have no empirical sense.

### A view of moderate empiricism

Being aware that mathematics can be done both as pure and as applied, moderate empiricists maintain that pure mathematics is an aprioristic discipline which needs no support from experience, nor need it fear that its assertions will ever be refuted by experience, simply because the terms of pure mathematics do not possess an empirical sense at all. As regards applied mathematics, on the other hand, it can be done, according to moderate empiricists, only as an empirical discipline. The axioms, that is to say the principal mathematical assertions which are accepted in mathematics without having been derived from other assertions, are, as far as applied mathematics is concerned, only hypotheses, whose logical consequences can be confirmed or refuted by confrontation with experience.

## A view of radical empiricism

Radical empiricism is an older doctrine, coming from the period when the distinction between pure and applied mathematics was unknown. Talking about mathematics and considering it to be an empirical science, radical empiricists had in mind applied mathematics and as far as it was concerned did not differ in their opinions from moderate empiricists, who also consider applied mathematics to be an empirical science. The form of mathematics now represented by the various branches of pure mathematics was simply unknown to the adherents of radical empiricism.

## Conventionalism

The adherents of moderate empiricism, considering applied mathematics to be an empirical science, often combined this view with the doctrine called conventionalism. The view that applied mathematics is an empirical science can be reduced to the assertion that if the terms occurring in mathematical statements are taken in their established meaning, then the truth or falsehood of these statements can be determined only by experience. If, for example, the geometrical terms contained in the statement 'the sum of the angles of a triangle is equal to 180 degrees' are taken in their colloquial meaning, the truth of the statement can be determined only by experience. Now this view, according to some thinkers reflecting on the character of mathematical assertions, requires some modifications. They point out that in many cases the colloquial meaning of mathematical terms does not provide us with a method which would enable us to decide about the truth of mathematical assertions on the basis of experience. Thus they express the opinion that with the colloquial understanding of mathematical terms some of its assertions – and what is at issue is first of all some geometrical assertions – cannot be decided by means of experience. They do not assert, however, that they can be decided independently of experience, that is *a priori*, but point out that the colloquial meaning of geometrical terms is not exact enough to permit us to decide about statements containing these terms in any way whatever. Insufficient exactness of the meaning of terms is often the reason why these statements are undecidable.

Let us take, for example, the word 'brook'. The colloquial meaning of this word provides us with a method which permits us, on the basis of experiential data when we look at moving water, to decide in many cases whether we should call it a brook or not. The Vistula at Warsaw cannot be called a brook, if this word is to be taken in its colloquial meaning; the Vistula at its sources, on the other hand, will undoubtedly be called a brook. When however we follow the course of the Vistula from its sources we shall find places about which we shall be unable to decide whether the Vistula at these places is a brook or not a brook any longer. We can measure the depth and the width of the Vistula at such a place but it will not help us to decide the question: is the Vistula a brook at this place? If, however, we agree that by 'brook' we shall understand 'a moving flow of water whose average annual width equals so-and-so many metres and whose depth is so-and-so many metres' after this agreement the previous difficulties will disappear; on the basis of experiential data we shall be able to decide at every place along the course of the Vistula whether it is, at this place, a brook or not.

Now according to some it is not only colloquial terms whose meaning is inexact but geometrical terms as well and in particular the meaning of the expression 'line $a$ is equal to line $b$'. They point out that with the colloquial meaning of this expression we are unable to determine on the basis of experiential data whether line $a$ is equal to line $b$ when the two lines are separated from each other. In order to settle this question we must make the meaning of this expression more exact by an agreement, that is a convention (*convenio* = I agree), as we have done with the word 'brook'. Depending on our agreement, experience will dictate this or that answer to the question about the equality of the two lines. The doctrine whose basic idea we have outlined here is called *conventionalism*.

Conventionalism is thus a modification of moderate empiricism. It agrees that the truth of assertions of applied mathematics can be decided only through experience. Conventionalism adds a further thesis to this one. It maintains that the truth of assertions of applied mathematics can be decided only by experience, but after we have made the colloquial sense of mathematical terms more exact by convention.

### A view of moderate apriorism: the teaching of Kant

Moderate apriorism holds a different view of the character of mathematical assertions. Its adherents when talking about mathematics have in mind, like radical empiricists, applied mathematics, that is the science which does not endow its terms with meaning with explicit definitions and axioms playing the part of implicit definitions but accepts the colloquial meaning of these terms and enriches its vocabulary and conceptual apparatus only by means of explicit definitions. Assertions of mathematics so understood and particularly its principal assumptions, that is the axioms, are thought by apriorists to be neither assertions which can be justified only by means of experience nor analytic statements, which would only elucidate the sense of the terms contained in them. The axioms of mathematics are, according to apriorists, synthetic *a priori* statements. Let us take, for example, the axiom of geometry which affirms that through a point lying outside a given line one and only one line can be drawn that is parallel to it. This axiom as a statement of applied mathematics is neither a component of an implicit definition endowing the geometrical terms it contains with sense nor is it only an elucidation of the colloquial sense of its terms; it is therefore a synthetic judgement. But it is not a synthetic judgement based on experience. What it affirms cannot be investigated experientially. Yet we accept this axiom with complete certainty and we feel entitled to do so. For it is enough to try to imagine the straight line and the point lying outside it to see at once that through this point we can draw one and only one line parallel to the given straight line. Pure intuition and not sense experience is a sufficient basis for giving the judgement without recourse to experience. The main representative of this view of the character of mathematical axioms was the German eighteenth-century philosopher Immanuel Kant.

Without entering into controversy, which would be out of place here with this – in our opinion incorrect – view of the aprioristic character of the assertions of applied mathematics, we shall mention only that it suffered a severe blow as a result of the development of mathematics in the nineteenth and twentieth centuries. In the nineteenth-century non-

Euclidean geometrics were constructed within the realm of pure mathematics in which the axiom mentioned above about parallel lines was replaced by axioms incompatible with it. The French scientist H. Poincaré, after an analysis in the spirit of conventionalism of these systems of non-Euclidean geometry, showed that each of these mutually incompatible systems of geometry, like the Euclidean system when considered as a branch of applied mathematics, can be made to agree with experience, if we make the meaning of the colloquial terms they contain more exact in a specific way. Finally, in the twentieth century, the creator of relativity theory, A. Einstein, has shown that, by choosing a non-Euclidean geometry as our basis, we arrive, through experience, at a system of physics simpler than what we would have obtained had we chosen the system of Euclidean geometry which Kant considered to be the only true geometry and to be *a priori* indubitable. For more detailed information on this subject, the reader must consult specialised literature.

To conclude these remarks about the dispute between apriorism and empiricism with regard to mathematical assertions, we shall point out another important problem that arises for any apriorism which accepts that the assertions of applied mathematics have the character of synthetic *a priori* assertions. Synthetic assertions of applied mathematics affirm what can be directly or indirectly confirmed or refuted by experience. For example, the assertion that the sum of the angles in a triangle is equal to two right angles if taken in its colloquial meaning, that is if treated as an assertion of applied mathematics, can be subjected to the test of experience by measuring the angles of a triangle and summing up our measurements. If we accept, as apriorism does, that the truth of this assertion is guaranteed *a priori,* then we are faced with an astonishing fact that we can *a priori,* that is beforehand and without any recourse to experience whatsoever, predict the results of future experiences. Without waiting for the results of our measurements of the angles of a triangle, we can predict beforehand what those results are going to be. However, this is not the kind of prediction of the result of future experiences which we deal with when, on the basis of the laws of physics or other natural sciences, we predict certain facts which experience will later confirm. The laws of physics and other natural sciences are themselves based on experience; predicting future facts on the basis of them, I predict the results of future experiences on the basis of past experiences. The laws of geometry are, however, according to apriorism, assertions which have nothing to do with experience whatsoever. When I predict future experiential facts on the basis of the laws of geometry, I predict them independently of all experience and I base these predictions on reason alone.

For empiricism of all varieties this problem does not exist. For empiricism considers all synthetic assertions of applied geometry to be empirical laws of the same kind as the laws of the natural sciences. Analytic geometrical assertions are as a matter of fact *a priori* assertions but they can be neither confirmed nor refuted by experience (cf. p. 28).

This is, however, a serious problem for apriorism which has to explain how it comes about that when we cut ourselves off from all experience, when we close our eyes, block our ears, etc. and do not take advantage of past experience, we can predict the result of future experiences by pure reason alone. Apriorism must explain the surprising harmony which occurs between reasoning detached from any experience and experience itself. In order to explain this fact Kant saw it to be necessary to admit that this harmony is to be explained by the fact that the objects with which we deal in experience are not independent of the mind but are created by it. The process of perception does not consist, according to Kant, only in passive reception of a reality independent of us, but is a creative process; in this process our minds, stimulated by a reality independent of us, produce those objects which we call the objects of perception. Those objects are not something genuinely real but are a kind of phantasms. The point is that the mind in producing these phantasms follows the same schemata which it follows in reasoning independent of all experience. This fact explains why simply from the schemata of the construction of objects given in experience we are able to give an account *a priori* without waiting for experience and why those aprioristic predictions will be confirmed by future experiences. Kant's hypothesis, which considers experiential objects, that is the objects which make up the nature that surrounds us, to be the creation of the mind, is one of the forms of idealism which will be discussed in later chapters of this book.

### The essence of a priori cognition according to phenomenologists

*A priori* cognition is the subject of detailed investigations by the well-known contemporary philosophical school called phenomenology, whose creator and main representative was the German philosopher Edmund Husserl. This thinker accepts a maxim, equivalent to that of empiricism, that all cognition which is more than merely verbal, explicating the sense of words, must be based on experience. But this maxim has a different meaning for Husserl from what it has for empiricists. The empiricists when they talk about experience have in mind sense-experience, in which physical objects and phenomena are given, or introspection, in which mental phenomena are given. Husserl points out, however, that there is another form of experience in which as directly as physical phenomena are given in sense-experience and mental pheno-mena in introspection, certain entities are given which do not belong to either the physical or the mental world. The physical and mental worlds together make up the world of real entities, as existing in time. Besides this real world there is, according to Husserl, a world of ideal entities which are timeless (we say 'there is' because Husserl himself teaches that it does not exist in the same sense as the real world). To this world belong ideas, that is the essences of things.

Husserl's 'essences of things' are rather mysterious, they correspond approximately to Platonic ideas (cf. p. 82 *et seq.*). The essence of a given thing, as an example of a given species, is just this species itself and, consequently, the essence of an object which I am now holding in my hand as I write, a pen, is the species 'pen'; the essence of a drawing, which is drawn on a sheet of paper lying in front of me which is square, is the species 'square' (square in general) etc. Now Husserl asserts that those essences of things can be given to us as directly as bodies are in sense perception. When I look at the red cloth covering my desk, I perceive this concrete thing with my senses but at the same time my mind is aware of what the essence of redness consists of. This awareness of the essence of redness is, according to Husserl, a form of immediate experience different from sense-experience. The differences between these two forms of experience is analysed by Husserl in detail. The experience in which the essences of things are purportedly given to us is called by Husserl 'intuition of essences' (*Wesensschau*). On the basis of this intuition of essences we can, according to Husserl, arrive at assertions which are indubitable, but which we could not arrive at through sense-experience. So, for example, the intuition of the essence of redness provides us with the certain knowledge that redness is inseparable from extension and, therefore, that every red thing must be extended. The assertion that what is red is extended is a general assertion and cannot be based on a particular sense-perception because that could support only the assertion that this red thing is extended. Nor is our assertion arrived at in an inductive way from many sense-perceptions, because inductive conclusions are not certain whereas our assertion is indubitable. The assertion that what is red is extended is not based on the analysis of the

43

meaning of the terms that are contained in it, it is not therefore an analytic assertion. It is thus an assertion independent of sense-experience and, consequently, an *a priori* assertion, yet, at the same time, it is not an analytic assertion and so it is synthetic *a priori*.

According to the phenomenologists the axioms of mathematics are only the verbal formulation of the knowledge acquired about numbers and other ideal mathematical entities by means of previous intuition of essences. Such expressions as 'natural number', 'point', 'straight line', 'plane', etc. are not names of real objects accessible to sense-experience. They are the names of ideal objects which can be given to us directly in that form of experience which the phenomenologists call the intuition of essences. Through this intuition of essences we get to know certain properties, relations, etc. of the ideal entities with which mathematics is concerned and in formulating axioms we give an account of the knowledge thus gained. By means of axioms we do not construct – phenomenologists insist – any ideal entities as some people suppose. Ideal entities can no more be created by human decree than real objects. The world of ideal entities subsists independently of our thought; it is the task of mathematics and other a priori sciences to explore this world. We explore it by deriving various conclusions from axioms by means of logical deduction. The axioms themselves are not plucked out of thin air, are not established by convention, but are the expression of the knowledge of ideal mathematical objects gained by the intuition of essence which is prior to all deduction. Mathematics based on axioms plucked from thin air, dictated by the whim of a scientist and not supported by the intuition of an essence, would, as a whole, hang in the air and thus would be a thing devoid of any cognitive value.

It is quite clear that these views of phenomenologists are concerned only with applied mathematics, that is, where the terms in its assertions are taken in their colloquial meaning.

Moderate empiricism asserts that the axioms of applied mathematics are accessible to empirical testing only if they are not analytic assertions. Phenomenology on the other hand ascribes to these non-analytic axioms the character of *a priori* judgements. In acknowledging the legitimacy of synthetic *a priori* judgements phenomenology puts itself on the side of moderate apriorism.

Without going into a more detailed critical analysis of the views of the phenomenologists we shall make one more remark which we cannot elaborate here more fully. What phenomenologists call the intuition of essences may also be called careful scrutiny of the meaning of words. Statements based on the latter only explicate the meaning of the terms contained in them and so are analytic statements. Hence the objections raised by phenomenologists to moderate empiricism are undermined.

## Rationalism and irrationalism

We shall now discuss the second pair of opposing tendencies: rationalism and irrationalism, in other words anti-irrationalism and irrationalism. Rationalist maxims occur frequently in the history of human thought. The moment of their greatest historical intensity and influence was in the eighteenth century when they were an essential feature of the ideology of the age of enlightenment. Rationalism proclaims the cult of rational knowledge – in opposition to irrationalism; the cult of knowledge gained in a natural way – as opposed to knowledge gained from supernatural sources; the cult of intellect – as opposed to emotion. However, all these formulations are general, not tangible enough, and can easily become the source of misunderstandings. The maxim of rationalism has hardly ever been formulated explicitly (that is in the way which rationalism would consider to be proper). Rationalism values cognition whose paradigm is scientific cognition or more precisely whose paradigms are the mathematical and natural sciences. It rejects cognition based on revelation, all divinations, forebodings, prophecies, crystal-gazing, etc. It is not easy, however, to say what distinguishes scientific cognition from cognition of those other kinds.

Perhaps scientific cognition can be characterised best by emphasising two requirements which it must satisfy. Scientific cognition is first such and only such content of thought as can be communicated to others in words understood literally, that is without metaphors, analogies and other half-measures for the transmission of thought. Secondly, only those assertions can pretend to the title of scientific cognition whose correctness or incorrectness can be decided in principle by anybody who finds himself in the appropriate external conditions. In a word, scientific cognition is that which is intersubjectively communicable and controllable.

It is just this intersubjectivity that seems to be characteristic of rational cognition. Rationalism, in valuing only rational cognition, amounts to recognising the worth only of intersubjectively communicable and controllable cognition. The motive from which rationalism values this kind of cognition alone is social. Rationalism proclaims that we can announce our convictions and call for their universal acceptance only when they can be clearly formulated in words and when everybody can (at least in principle) assure himself of their correctness or incorrectness. The point here is, first, to protect society from the domination of the meaningless cliché which often has a strong emotional resonance and, because of this, influences individuals and whole social groups; and, secondly, in order to give protection from the uncritical acceptance of views proclaimed by their adherents sometimes with the full force of conviction but which are inaccessible to testing by others and thus might be suspected to be false. The point is to protect society from nonsense and falsehood. This postulate seems as sensible as the requirement of railway administration which allows a passenger to travel only when he can produce a valid ticket and not when, although he has paid for the ticket, he does not want to show it. Paying for the journey corresponds in this comparison to the truth of an assertion; readiness to show the ticket corresponds to the possibility that anyone can become assured as to whether the assertion is valid or not.

Rational cognition, however, pays a high price for its intersubjective character. It becomes schematic, abstract and it loses its intimate contact with the object. We shall explain this by means of an example. Everyone possesses detailed knowledge of his own experiences. When I experience a pain it is given to me in all its concreteness, in all its nuances. Let us attempt, however, to express what we know about our own pain without metaphors, in unequivocal terms. We shall notice at once how little we can express of what we know ourselves about our pain without metaphors. We may perhaps indicate the place in which the pain is located, we shall be able to describe approximately the intensity of the pain. Beyond this we have to use metaphors, we describe pain as throbbing, pricking, burning, sharp, blunt, etc. (these are metaphors: 'as if I were pricked with a needle, as if I were burned' etc.). But in spite of these metaphors we are unable by means of words alone to provide anyone with the knowledge about our pain we possess ourselves. This inadequacy of our speech is less striking when we attempt to convey fully concrete knowledge about objects and events given to us in direct experience, when we use it to describe objects given to us in sensory experience. But it is apparent even here: when I want to describe the colour of a given object and I call it 'red', or 'light red', or mention a more specific colour, this description will always fit a number of different nuances of this colour. Thus what can be conveyed to others of our knowledge about the objects given us in direct experience is only a schema, is always an abstraction which the

47

hearer must fill out with concrete content on his own responsibility and it will not necessarily be identical with the content we attempted to convey by means of the words used in our description. What can be conveyed of our knowledge of objects in words cannot replace the direct experience of those objects. It will always preserve a certain distance and it will not express such an intimate contact with them as the contact which we establish with them by perceiving them (if we have in mind objects of the physical world) or by experiencing them (if we have in mind our own mental states).

Those who oppose rationalism point out that rational cognition is schematic, abstract and lacks intimate contact with objects. The opponents of rationalism recognise the significance of rational cognition for practice and action but they deny that it has the completeness which is characteristic of the cognition achieved through immediate contact with objects and inexpressible in intersubjective words. They contend that this inexpressible cognition should be given at least as much respect as rational cognition. In recent times the main opponent of rationalism was the French philospher Bergson, who opposes to rational cognition (which he calls analysis) intuition, which is inexpressible in words but which enables us to know reality itself without restriction and not only its schema.

The opponents of rationalism are called irrationalists. Representatives of irrationalism appear very early in the history of thought. To start with, mystics of all kinds belong here. By mystics we mean people who have peculiar kinds of experiences called mystical ecstasies. In these experiences they undergo revelations in which they gain (not by means of reasoning and scrupulous observation) subjective certainty, most often as to the existence of a deity, they experience its existence directly as if face to face, they receive direct instructions, admonitions and orders from it. People who undergo such experiences cannot be argued out of their conviction of the certainty of knowledge gained in states of ecstasy; and they are even less shaken by the judgements of rationalists about their faith. The certainty of their knowledge is too great, the new horizons, the new vision of the world, the fullness of life they gain through this knowledge are too valuable for them to give it up. They cannot be persuaded that since they cannot justify their thesis sufficiently they should restrain themselves from affirming it. It is thus in vain that rationalists try to convince the mystic and to restrain him from fulfilling his apostolic mission. However, the voice of the rationalist is a sound social reaction, it is an act of self-defence by society against the dangers of being dominated by uncontrollable forces among which may be both a saint proclaiming a revelation as well as a madman affirming the products of his sick imagination and finally a fraud who wants to convert others to his views for the sake of his egoistic and unworthy purposes. It is better to rely on the safe but modest nourishment of reason than, in fear of missing the voice of 'Truth', to let oneself be fed with all sorts of uncontrollable nourishment which may more often be poisonous than healthy and beneficial.

# 4

## The problem of the limits of knowledge

### Two meanings of transcendence

The problem mentioned in the title of this chapter is that of whether the cognising subject can go beyond itself in the act of cognition, whether it can transcend its own limits. The equivalent in Latin of the English phrase 'go beyond' is the word *transcendere*, hence the problem which we now sketch is called the problem of transcendence and objects lying beyond the limits of the cognising subject are called transcendental objects. When we ask whether the cognising subject can go beyond its own limits in the act of cognition we are asking whether cognition of reality that is transcendental in relation to the cognising subject is possible. But what is meant by reality that is transcendental in relation to a given subject? There are at least two different meanings of this term and because of this the problem of the limits of cognition has at least two interpretations.

On the first interpretation by the transcendental object, that is external to the cognising subject, is meant every object which is not the subject's own mental experience. When we ask whether the cognising subject can go beyond its own limits, whether in other words it can arrive in the act of cognition at a reality transcendental to it, we ask – on this first interpretation – *whether the cognising subject is capable of knowing anything that is not its own mental experience.* This is the first interpretation of the problem of the limits of knowledge. Our own mental experiences of a given object are called immanent products of the subject (from the Latin *in* and *maneo* = I remain inside). Because of this the first version of our problem which is concerned with whether the cognising subject can go beyond its own immanent sphere in a cognitive act is called the problem of immanent limits of cognition. One who answers the question affirmatively and, consequently, recognises that the subject is capable of going beyond its own immanent sphere in its cognitive acts is called an *immanent epistemological realist*. One who denies that the subject is capable of going beyond its own immanent sphere in its cognitive acts is called an *immanent epistemological idealist*.

The second interpretation of the problem of the limits of knowledge is connected with a second sense of the expression 'transcendent object'. In this second sense by transcendent objects we mean objects which really exist as opposed to objects of thought which do not really exist. For the man who does not philosophise, among objects which really exist and are not merely constructions of thought, and therefore are – in the second sense of the word – transcendent, are to be included, for example, the earth with everything that is and happens on it, all the stars and further mental subjects together with their experiences. Among objects of thought which do not really exist, the man who does not philosophise includes, for example, mythical beings, fauns and nymphs, fictional characters, events imagined by poets, and so on. Some philosophers, however, are inclined to draw different boundaries between what really exists and what is only a construction of thought; they regard the physical and mental worlds, which are considered in everyday life to be the truest reality, as a certain kind of constructions of thought. True reality for them, the world of transcendent beings, consists of some unknowable 'things in themselves' of which we know nothing and can say nothing.

The second interpretation of the problem of the limits of knowledge is connected with the second sense of the term 'transcendent object' we have just discussed. The problem here is *whether really existing objects are accessible to cognition or whether cognition can be concerned only with constructions of thought that do not really exist.* The philosophical trend which asserts that really existing objects are not accessible to cognition and that cognition can be concerned only with constructions of thought is called *transcendental epistemological idealism.*★ The trend according to which cognition can arrive at true reality is called *transcendental epistemological realism.*

Now that we have sketched the two interpretations of the problem of the limits of cognition and connected with them the trends of epistemological realism and idealism, we shall go on to analyse them in more detail.

## Immanent epistemological idealism

The British philosopher of the eighteenth century George Berkeley is considered to be the classical representative of immanent idealism. It is usually thought that in the process of sensory perception we become acquainted with extramental, that is non-immanent, objects. Berkeley analyses this view critically. What do I perceive by sight, asks Berkeley, when I look at the sheet of paper on which I am writing? I perceive a white rectangular surface, partly covered with blue lines. This surface and only this surface is the object of my perception, at least the immediate object of my perception, that is the object I am really seeing, and not the one which I

★ The two terms 'transcendent' and 'transcendental' should not be confused. The explanation of the latter term, introduced into philosophy by Kant, will be given later (cf. p. 59).

suppose to exist on the basis of what I really see. But what is this white surface which is the only object of my perception? Is it something objective independent of my perceptual apparatus? If this were so it would not have changed as the the result of changes in my perceptual apparatus. But the contrary is the case. It will double when I slightly press one of my eyes with my finger. It will turn from white to green if I interrupt my looking at it and go to a room lit with red lights and then return to look again at it in white light (following contrast). The inspected surface becomes different when I look at it from a short distance and still different again when I look at it from far away; different when if I am short-sighted I look at it through glasses, and different when I look at it with the naked eye. All this proves, according to Berkeley, that this white surface which I see when I look at the sheet of paper is my subjective impression and nothing else. Because I do not really perceive anything with my eyes but this white surface the only object of sensory perception is my own impression, a certain kind of experience, a certain immanent product.

Berkeley's immanent idealism is not carried through completely. His idealistic thesis does not embrace all cognition but is limited to sensory perception, asserting that in perception nothing but our own impressions can be given to us and thus nothing but mental experiences. Apart from sensory perceptions Berkeley also recognises other forms of cognition which can go beyond the experiences of the cognising subject. An example of cognition which goes beyond its subjects' own experiences is – according to Berkeley – the cognition of our own soul and of the souls of others which Berkeley does not identify with the mental experiences of the cognising subject.

Another British philosopher of the eighteenth century, David Hume, goes a step further and extends the thesis of immanent epistemological idealism, which Berkeley limited to sense-perception alone, to the inner perception by means of which he thinks we gain self-knowledge, the awareness of the soul or self as well. Just as Berkeley asked what is really perceived by means of our senses, so Hume asked what is really perceived in inner experience. To this question Hume answers that in inner experience we are given no more than our own mental states; in this experience a self which is different from these mental states is not given to us. If the words 'self' or 'soul' are to denote something that is given to us in inner experience then it cannot denote anything but the stream of our mental states. The soul, as something different from this stream of mental states, as something that is supposed to be a substratum of these states, or their subject, is not given in any experience. Hume thus asserts that in inner experience we know nothing besides our own mental states, we do not go beyond the immanent sphere.

## Perception and its object

The fundamental basis of immanent idealism is its view of the relation between the cognising subject and the object of cognition. In perceiving, for example, the relationship between the cognising subject and the object of perception consists, according to Berkeley, in the fact that this object itself becomes 'the content of consciousness', that is to say it simply becomes a mental experience. If we carry the analysis further and distinguish between the act and content of experience, we can say that the perceived object becomes – according to Berkeley and other immanent idealists – the content of experience.

The attacks of epistemological realism on Berkeley's and Hume's idealism start with criticism of their view about the relationship between the subject and the object of perception. The relationship of the object of perception and in general of the object of cognition to the cognising subject does not, according to realists, consist in the fact that this object, at the time when it is apprehended by the subject, simply enters into the subject and becomes his experience (or eventually becomes the content of this experience). The relationship is quite different. In the act of cognition the subject goes, as it were, beyond itself directing itself to something that is not its own content. And so, for instance, when I perceive this sheet of paper I have in mind something that does not have only the one side that is directed towards me but another side as well (which I do not see in the same sense as I see the front side), I perceive something that also has a certain weight, a certain chemical composition, etc. All this does not become the content of my consciousness; the content of my consciousness is only the white surface appearing before me and serving as the point of departure for my act of perception, in which through this content, as if through a gun-sight, my mind aims at something that is beyond consciousness. This relationship between the cognising subject and the object of cognition which we have tried to describe metaphorically is called *the intentional relation*.

For this relationship to obtain it is not sufficient that a sensory content should appear in consciousness (for example, this white shape in the perception of a piece of paper). The cognising subject must also perform a number of operations in which certain concepts also play a role, operations which do not have a passive, receptive character, but which also possess an active, spontaneous character. It is because of these acts that 'objectivisation' takes place, that is the opposition of the cognising subject and the object of cognition.

Now since to perceive an object does not mean the same as to make this object the content of consciousness, since to perceive an object does not mean the same as to force it into the subject, the main argument of Berkeley fails, the argument which he uses to show that only the contents of consciousness, that is mental experiences, can be objects of perception.

The analysis of the perceptual process, the description of all these thought-operations, participating in it and leading to the opposition in the act of perception of the subject of perception to the object towards which its intention is directed, is one of the most important problems from the frontier region between psychology and the theory of knowledge. This problem is sometimes called the problem of the constitution of the object of perception.

To draw attention to the fact that the knowing subject does not behave passively in the act of perception by merely admitting the perceived object into itself but that, on the contrary, the knowing subject behaves actively in perception, that is to say that the perceived object is constituted by the mind, is to pose the question whether the object of perception is not on this account merely a construction of thought and not something real, independent of the knowing subject. The theory of knowledge is concerned with this problem which is called 'transcendental idealism'. To this problem we now turn our attention.

### Transcendental epistemological idealism

Whenever one thinks, one thinks about something; whenever one perceives, one perceives something; whenever one imagines, one imagines something. Now this something about which one thinks, which one perceives, which one imagines, is usually called the *intentional object* of thought, perception, imagination, etc. We do not consider all the objects of our thought, imagination, etc. as really existing. Some of them (for example, fauns and centaurs) are denied real existence and are considered to be fictions; only some of the objects of our thought, imagination, etc. are recognised as really existing.

When we distinguish fiction from reality we apply certain criteria. The most important of them is the criterion of experience; we usually appeal to experience when we have to decide whether something is a fiction or a reality.

Now the theory of knowledge inquires whether the criteria which we apply when distinguishing between fiction and reality lead to the recognition as real of only such objects as really exist. Perhaps even the objects which satisfy these criteria are also merely constructions of thought and not realities existing independently of the mind. This doubt may arise when we consider that man can recognise as real only what he is able to present to himself, that in general which he can somehow think about. But our capacity for presenting things to ourselves is limited by certain forms of imagination and thinking that are inseparably linked with human nature. So, for example, the fact that we perceive and imagine objects as coloured we owe to the organisation of our senses. If our eyes had been differently constructed, the world might not have appeared coloured but something else. The same applies, according to some, to shapes also. If our cognitive capacities were differently organised, we should not have perceived the world – they argue – in spatial forms but somehow differently. However, not only our senses but our minds too are limited in their capacity for presenting objects to themselves. Our minds operate with such concepts as their organisation allows. If they were organised differently, they would have operated with different concepts and therefore would have constructed the conceptual model of the world differently. Now since what is possible to our minds is limited by the organisation of their cognitive capacities and our minds cannot present everything to themselves but only what is allowed by their organisation and regardless of what reality actually is, they cannot transcend these limits, we should at least admit the possibility that the organisation of our minds will never allow us to present a reality independent of the mind to ourselves and that our minds are constantly occupied with their own constructions. If this were the case even the objects represented by the mind, which are accepted by it as real according to the criterion of experience, that is the criterion which enables us to distinguish fiction from reality, would have been its own constructions since it can conceive nothing that is not its own construction.

There have been some philosophers, indeed, who not only thought this a possibility but also thought that they had found arguments proving that it is the case. According to them the world which we recognise as real, even when we apply the most scrupulous criterion of experience, is not a true reality independent of our minds but is only a construction of these minds. Our minds are not capable of knowing a world that exists independently of them, that is the world of 'things in themselves', but are doomed to constant confinement to their own constructions. This is the thesis of the kind of epistemological idealism which is called transcendental idealism.

The adherents of this kind of idealism deny, therefore, that experience (or any other criterion which we use in practice to distinguish fiction from reality) leads us to the recognition as real of those objects which exist independently of our minds, that is which are something other than intentional objects. Nevertheless, the idealists did not consider judgements asserted on the basis of experience to be false. As a matter of fact, the idealists do not adhere to the classical definition of truth; they identify the truth of cognition with agreement with selected criteria. As such a selected criterion they consider the evidence of experience together with the criterion of internal harmony and universal agreement (cf. pp. 12-15). So they do not consider all knowledge based on experience to be false: nor do they think that the world which is presented by this knowledge as reality is wholly made of fictions and illusions. On the contrary, they make their fundamental distinction between what is supported by experience and what is denied by experience. They call fiction and illusion only what could be rejected by experience. Those entities which are supported by experience as the criterion of truth are called *phenomena*. They claim that to say that phenomena have empirical reality is to say nothing more than they are supported by the criteria of experience, internal harmony and universal agreement and that therefore these phenomena belong to the world of intentional objects, universally accepted by everyone; they deny that these phenomena have an existence independent of our minds, that is that they are something more than merely conceived objects, that is intentional objects.

### Kant as representative of transcendental idealism

A representative of the kind of idealism just discussed was Kant. He arrives at his position in two ways. The gist of the first could be presented in the following way: Kant asserts that *a priori*, without any recourse to experience, we arrive at certain assertions which in principle could be refuted by experience (because they are not analytic judgements but only synthetic) but which are later constantly confirmed by experience and about which we are certain beforehand that they will never be refuted by experience. Among such assertions are, Kant holds, the propositions of geometry, for example the judgement that the sum of two sides of a triangle must be greater than its third side. It is sufficient to visualise a triangle and imagine that two of its sides turn around the ends of its base and fall on it. It is clear at once that they will cover the whole base and partly overlap each other and that therefore their sum is greater than the third side (cf. pp. 29–30). In order to assert this one does not have to appeal to experience, pure intuition is enough. However, these assertions gained without recourse to experience are never refuted by it. How can we explain how, without waiting for experience and therefore *a priori*, we know certain general laws governing the world that is revealed to us in experience? Kant formulates this question as: how are synthetic *a priori* judgements possible?

This is the fundamental question which Kant poses in his main epistemological treatise *The Critique of Pure Reason*. The inquiries which aim at a solution of this problem are called by Kant *transcendental inquiries*. He himself finds the solution in idealism of a certain kind. Because of this, this kind of idealism is called transcendental.

Kant's solution to the problem could be sketched in the following way. If experience had revealed a true reality to us and not merely our constructions of thought, the harmony between the synthetic judgements our minds arrive at *a priori* and experience would have been incomprehensible indeed, an extraordinary coincidence. This will not be the case if we admit that the entities presented to us by experience are also constructions of thought. It will then become comprehensible that our minds without waiting for experience can arrive *a priori* at knowledge of general principles according to which it itself constructs objects in the act of perception, therefore the objects given to it in experience. In order to solve the problem of synthetic *a priori* judgements we have to admit, according to Kant, that objects given to us in experience are only constructions of our minds and are not a reality independent of them (that is to say they are not things in themselves, *Dinge an sich*).

But Kant also attempts to justify his idealistic thesis in another way. He analyses the way in which our minds arrive, in the act of perception, at the opposition between them and perceived objects, that is he analyses the problem of the constitution of the object of perception. This analysis shows that spatial forms and concepts (categories) participate in the constitution of the objects of perception. Because on the other hand Kant shows the subjective character of these forms and concepts, consequently the way in which objects of perception are constituted itself serves according to Kant as a proof that perceived objects are only constructions of our minds and do not really exist. Kant's arguments about this topic are difficult and complex and cannot be concisely presented so as to be fully intelligible.

## Realism

Against transcendental idealism, realism advances the thesis of the real existence of objects that are given to us in experience. In the dispute with idealism the realist attacks its arguments. The most frequent targets of criticism are the contentions of idealism about the constitution of objects of perception. The realists attempt to explain this constitution in such a way that it does not lead to idealistic consequences. Most often, however, the realists reject as a baseless presumption the pretension of the theory of knowledge to give a judgement about the validity of the criterion of experience. They contend that the criteria which idealists use in their reasonings are no more trustworthy than the criterion of experience which idealists criticise. According to many realists, experience justifies our faith in reality and in the existence of a world given to us in experience but independent of the subject so strongly that no epistemological criticism could undermine it, or strengthen it.

A still more severe criticism claims not only that transcendental idealism is false but claims further the whole problem posed by idealism is devoid of sense. In this problem the following terms occur: 'reality existing independently of our minds', 'object which is not only conceived but exists independently of our minds'. The point is that these terms are unfortunately insufficiently clarified. Some even assert that they have no sense whatever. This is the objection to idealism and the objection even to the problem posed by it launched by thinkers from the school of positivism which we shall now consider.

## Positivism

Positivism also is concerned with the problem of the limits of knowledge but it attaches a different meaning to it from the one we met in the dispute between idealism and realism.

Positivism accepts the fundamental thesis of empiricism according to which we can know reality only on the basis of experience. However, positivism goes even further and supplements this thesis with another assertion: that the object of knowledge can be only what is given or can be given in experience. Affirming this positivists hold a certain view not only about the sources of knowledge but also about the limits of knowledge. The positivist thesis does not follow from the empiricist thesis taken by itself. From the fact that knowledge of reality must be based on experience it does not follow that knowledge cannot be of something that is not given in experience. We can assume that the opposite is the case, that starting from experience we can by means of reasoning ascend higher and arrive at knowledge of something that is not and cannot be given in experience. This possibility seems to be confirmed by various physical theories which, although based on experience, arrive at knowledge about electromagnetic waves, electrons, protons, etc. which are not perceived by anybody and could not be perceived. Now positivism, without denying the validity of these physical theories, maintains that assertions occurring in them that refer to something inaccessible to immediate perception only appear to refer to something that transcends experience. According to the positivists these physical assertions are only shorthand, which when they are expounded in full, translate into statements referring to things accessible in immediate experience. So, for example, a statement affirming that electric current flows through a wire is not to be understood according to positivists in such a way that would imply that imperceptible and unimaginable electrons are moving along the wire; the proper sense of the statement that electric current flows through a wire is different. This statement, according to the positivists, asserts only that because of the condition of the wire in appropriate circumstances certain specific and perceptible phenomena occur and so, for instance, that if the ends of the wire are connected to an amperometer its needle changes its position, if they are submerged in an electrolytic solution electrolytic phenomena will occur, if we measure the temperature of the water we shall find that it rises, etc. In a word according to the positivists the statement about the flow of current in the wire asserts only the possibility (in appropriate circumstances) of the occurrence of all these perceptible phenomena which serve as criteria in answering the question whether the current flows through the wire.

Asserting their thesis about the limits of knowledge positivists oppose all the pretensions of the human mind to knowledge of any supersensory world. Because metaphysics is often conceived as the science of a supersensory world positivists thus direct their criticism first of all against metaphysics so conceived. According to the positivists, everything that we can know about reality is exhausted by the particular natural sciences. *There is no other knowledge about the world, only what is provided by these sciences.* According to them, the task of philosophy is not to ascend above these sciences and to search for a deeper knowledge of reality than any that the natural sciences provide us with, but *its task is simply that of making syntheses and systematisations of the results of these sciences.* Beyond this philosophy can and should reflect on scientific knowledge, *become the theory of science.*

The foundations of positivist thought can be found in the

British philosopher D. Hume, already mentioned (eighteenth century); they were developed systematically by the French nineteenth-century thinker Auguste Comte. In the history of philosophy positivism has taken a variety of shades: idealist, realist and neutral. It depended on the view taken as to what is the object of perception. Some positivists, for example Hume, thought that the objects of external perception are only the contents of our impressions, of inner perception – or on the other hand our own mental states. Since according to the basic positivist thesis our knowledge cannot transcend what can be perceived, knowledge for these positivists is limited to knowledge of the world of our impressions and our mental states. Other positivists have taken the realistic view that objects of perception are independent of the subject perceiving them. Some others again have contended that we perceive complexes of certain elements: colours, scents, sounds, tastes, etc. out of which both bodies and the stream of consciousness can be constructed, but which themselves (that is if taken in abstraction from the complex being considered) are neither mental nor physical but are neutral elements and can exist even if they are not perceived.

The Austrian scientist E. Mach, who lived at the turn of the nineteenth and twentieth centuries, asserted as did Berkeley, that the bodies given to us in experience are only complexes of colours, sounds, scents, etc. What, for example, is the pencil I am perceiving at the moment? It is something that has a long, narrow, yellow surface which I can see at the moment, a hexagonal surface of the colour of wood, with a black point in the middle which I could perceive if I looked at the pencil along its length and, further, all those sights which I should have seen if I had looked at the pencil from various directions and, furthermore, those sights which would have been revealed to me if the outer layers of the pencil had been removed so that I could look at its inner layers. Apart from this there are other aspects of the pencil which would have appeared to me if I had examined it with other senses than sight, its cool smooth surface if I had touched it, etc. But what is the self, that is my own soul? To this question Mach answers, as Hume did, that our selves are nothing more than bundles of impressions, memories, thoughts, feelings, desires, etc. Among the elements of which my self is made there are some elements whose complexes are bodies. According to Mach – as we have already said – bodies are nothing else but colours, sounds, scents, etc. But what are these colours, sounds, scents, but what is given to us immediately when we look at objects, what we have called impressions. Colours, sounds, scents, etc. are therefore elements which if considered as components of complexes of which the self or the soul is made are called impressions, on the other hand if considered as components of other complexes of elements, namely those which are bodies, are called properties of these bodies. These colours, sounds, scents, etc., considered in abstraction from both memories, feelings, desires which together make the stream of consciousness, and from the complexes which make up bodies, are neither mental nor physical. Taken in abstraction, they are neutral elements which can equally be called physical or mental. These expressions ('physical' or 'mental') can be applied to them only as components of this or that complex.

The well-known contemporary British philosopher Bertrand Russell has advocated views similar to those of Mach which we have just discussed.

## Neopositivism

Contemporary neopositivism has emerged from the neutral positivism of Mach but, in the course of its development, it gave up Mach's position and accepted a realist one in regard to the objects of perception. In its further development it has also given up the fundamental thesis of positivism that limits knowledge to perceptible objects. It has retained only the empiricist thesis, in the form of moderate empiricism, according to which all knowledge which does not consist of the elucidation of the meaning of expressions, and consequently is not expressible in analytic statements, must be based on experience. Not only do the neopositivists think that all synthetic statements, if they cannot be either confirmed or refuted by experience, are baseless (in this they agree with moderate empiricism), but they go even further and consider such statements as devoid of sense. According to Kant, metaphysics should be made only of synthetic statements which are not under the control of experience and consequently of such judgements as according to the neopositivists are devoid of any sense whatever. Hence the devastating criticism by neopositivists of metaphysics which is condemned and considered to be made up of expressions without meaning, to be futile talk without any sense.

In their anti-metaphysical attitude the neopositivists agree with one of the fundamental theses of the older positivism. They also agree with positivism that all knowledge of reality is contained in the empirical sciences, in physics, geology, astronomy, history, etc. Apart from the knowledge contained in particular empirical sciences, there is no other knowledge of reality of the kind to which metaphysics pretends. Writing off metaphysics and together with it normative ethics, they retain for philosophy the theory of knowledge as its sole field of inquiry; psychological elements, that is inquiries concerned with cognitive processes, are excluded from the theory of knowledge. There remain only the investigation of cognitive results and thus an investigation whose objects are scientific assertions. Scientific assertions, however, the neopositivists identify with statements and thus with certain linguistic expressions in which these assertions are uttered. Because of this the task of philosophy is made even more precise: philosophy can be only the theory of scientific language. Having determined the task of philosophy in this way, the neopositivists proceed to cultivate this area fruitfully. They cultivate the theory of scientific language. This theory, however, is far removed from what linguists study. The theory of scientific knowledge, as it is conceived by positivists, is identical with logic in its contemporary form. So this logic is the main realm in which neopositivism flourishes and to which it has made considerable contributions. But the cultivation of contemporary logic is not the monopoly of the neopositivists. It can be cultivated by those who do not share their views. The main achievements in this field do not come from neopositivists, as a matter of fact.

In spite of their negative attitude to all philosophy – except for the part which can be confined within the limits recognised and cultivated by the neopositivist theory of language – they do not really write off the remaining philosophical problems but attempt to show that they have been badly formulated. They were formulated as if they were concerned with things and in this form, because of their unclarity and ambiguity they were hopeless, whereas, as a matter of fact, they were not concerned with things but with words about things. In the history of philosophy much attention has been devoted to consideration of the essence of things. It was asked, for example, what is the essence of man, the essence of plants, the essence of animals, etc. All explanations of what is meant by the word 'essence' were however nebulous and intangible. Now neopositivists point out that this problem has been badly formulated. Those who asked about the essence of man (plants, animals) were not interested in pointing out something that is present in particular people (plants, animals) and is purportedly their essence; they were really interested in the meaning of the word 'man' (the word 'plant', the word 'animal'). The problem discussed here was therefore not concerned with things (people, plants, animals) but with words denoting these things. Thus the traditional problem of philosophy concerned with the essence of things, once it has been formulated in a proper way, becomes a problem about language and in this form it finds its place in the theory of language to which neopositivists attempt to limit philosophy. By paraphrasing various other problems of traditional philosophy in a similar way, that is by replacing problems concerned with things by problems concerned with words denoting these things, these problems can be accommodated in their new form in the philosophical programme of the neopositivists.

In their general attitude neopositivists are – as we have already mentioned – far away from the idealist version of positivism represented for example by Hume and they do not in the least suppose that mental phenomena only can be objects of knowledge.

They proclaim a programme called physicalism which affirms that the proper objects of knowledge are physical objects, that is bodies. Physicalism demands that the assertions of all the sciences should be reducible to the physicalistic language and so to assertions about bodies. Those assertions which cannot be reduced to the physicalist language do not, according to the neopositivists, satisfy the fundamental requirements laid down for scientific assertions: they are not intersubjectively communicable or testable. All assertions of psychology which refer to mental subjects and phenomena, as well as all assertions in the humanistic disciplines, if they are to have the character of scientific assertions, must be reducible to physicalist assertions. The postulate of physicalism brings neopositivism close to materialism.

# 5

## *The relation of the theory of knowledge to the other philosophical sciences*

The problems of the theory of knowledge that have been discussed above are regarded as classical. They are not all the problems which are included in the theory of knowledge. Among them are many problems from the boundary between the theory of knowledge and the part of logic called theory of science and methodology. The theory of science is concerned with science conceived as a system of scientific assertions and thus with already completed results. Methodology on the other hand deals with procedures, with the methods of doing science. The theory of science is concerned with the elements of which science is composed (assertions, scientific terms) and with the structures built out of them (proof, theory, etc.). Methodology inquires into methods of proof, experimentation, solutions of problems, explanation, testing, etc. Now in both these disciplines there are problems which can be included in the theory of knowledge. Among such problems are, for example, problems concerned with the validity of different scientific methods, e.g. the problem of the validity of inductive and deductive methods, the problem about the role of conventions (that is arbitrary solutions) in scientific knowledge and some others. Problems are often discussed in the domain of methodology and the theory of science which are the application of classical epistemological problems to specific parts of this or that science.

For all these reasons there is no sharp boundary between the theory of knowledge on the one hand and the theory of science and methodology on the other.

There are also very close connections between the theory of knowledge and metaphysics. To a great extent metaphysical inquiries consist of drawing conclusions about the nature of reality from this or that epistemological view. We shall analyse these connections in detail in the chapter devoted to metaphysics.

# Part II

# Metaphysics

# 6

## The origin of the term 'metaphysics' and the division of problems

### The origin of the word 'metaphysics'

Metaphysics, the second main philosophical discipline, owes its name to purely accidental circumstances. It was coined by Aristotle's pupils when ordering his works. Aristotle, one of the most outstanding Greek philosophers (fourth century B.C.), used the term 'philosophy' in its original etymological meaning (cf. p. 3), that is to say used it as equivalent to the term 'science'. Because of this he talked about different philosophies in the same sort of way as we talk today about different sciences. Now among various 'philosophies' Aristotle distinguished one as the most basic of all and called it first philosophy (*prote philosophia*). The task of this first philosophy was the investigation of the first principles of everything, of whatever exists. As the second science, that is the second philosophy, Aristotle considered natural science to which he devoted a number of works under the common title physics (*physica; phusis,* that is nature). After Aristotle's death his pupils when ordering his works placed the books of Aristotle devoted to this 'first philosophy' after his books about nature, that is after physics. Because of this the books about this first philosophy were called 'those that follow the books about nature' (*ta meta ta physica*) or, concisely in

Latin: *metaphysica*. In this purely accidental way the term 'metaphysics' was coined to describe books devoted to first philosophy.

In the books devoted to 'the first principles of being' Aristotle treats, among other things, God as an entity standing beyond nature. The fact that books devoted to first philosophy investigated what stands beyond nature became the reason that later different etymological interpretations were given of the term 'metaphysics'. Metaphysics came to be considered as the science which treats what is supernatural. Examining the content of investigations which in the course of human thought were called metaphysics, we can say that indeed supernatural topics such as God and the after-life were included within the scope of metaphysical inquiries. But they were not the sole topic of metaphysics.

## The division of metaphysical problems

The richness of the themes contained in metaphysics is so great and its problems are often so elusive that it is not easy to characterise metaphysics by means of a single formula that would exhaust its scope. Traditional characterisations of metaphysics are either very general or too narrow and fail to exhaust the themes contained in traditional metaphysics. As an example of too general a characterisation of metaphysics may be given the description of it as the discipline which attempts to formulate a view of the world or as the most general discipline about being. It is to characterise metaphysics too narrowly to describe it as a synthesis of knowledge about nature or as a science attempting to reveal the true reality hidden behind the illusory veil of phenomena presented to the senses, that is to say as a science about things-in-themselves. We shall therefore give up the attempt to provide a unitary description of metaphysics and we shall limit ourselves to the analysis of problems which have traditionally been included in metaphysics. We shall divide metaphysical problems into four groups. There is first ontology, secondly there are problems deriving from the investigation of knowledge, thirdly there are problems deriving from the investigation of nature, and fourthly there are problems deriving from religion and ethics. Each of these groups of problems will be discussed separately.

# 7

## *Ontology*

### The tasks of ontology

Etymologically the term 'ontology' derives from the Greek word *on*, that is from the present participle of the verb *einai* which is equivalent to the verb 'be'. Literally, therefore, *on* is equivalent to 'being'; the participle *on* prefixed with an article *to on* takes the noun form 'that which is', consequently 'anything'. Thus 'ontology', etymologically speaking, is the science of that which is, the science whose assertions are concerned with anything. According to this etymology, ontology is supposed to be the most general science whose assertions are applicable to everything that there is. It is in this way that Aristotle characterised the tasks of his first philosophy, the philosophical discipline later called metaphysics. The term 'ontology' is often used interchangeably with the term 'metaphysics' and the two words are used as synonyms.

However, a different meaning of the term is now being developed, mainly under the influence of the phenomenologists. Phenomenologists call all inquiries about the essence of things 'ontology' which according to them is to be carried on by means of the intuition of essences (*Wesensschau*) discussed on pp. 42–4. In investigating the 'essence of something', for example the essence of things in general, the essence of body, the essence of properties, the essence of relations, etc., I attempt to answer the question: 'what is a thing', 'what is a body', 'what are properties', 'what is a relation' etc. Answers to questions of this kind are definitions of the terms 'thing', 'body', 'property', 'relation' which have the following structure: 'a body is so and so'. These definitions do not have the character of proposals, are not presented as arbitrary postulations as to the way in which the words are to be used, but assume that these words already have definite meanings in our language; these definitions claim to be true statements providing that their terms have a definite meaning already. Definitions of this kind are called real definitions. Now, giving up phenomenological terminology, we can describe the task of ontology as *a search for real definitions of certain terms which are based on apprehension of the meaning ascribed to these terms in the language from which they are taken.* The terms whose real definitions ontology attempts to provide are usually taken from a technical language in which philosophical investigations are carried on but also partly from colloquial language.

The tasks of ontology are not exhausted by providing real definitions for these terms. Sometimes, without reaching these definitions, ontology is satisfied with affirming certain statements which are arrived at by apprehension of the meaning of the relevant terms, that is by the analysis of concepts which underlie these meanings. Because these concepts are usually very general (for example, the concept of thing, the concept of a property, the concept of a relation, etc.), the assertions at which ontology arrives through the analysis of these concepts are also of a very general character. Because of their generality they approach the description which Aristotle gave of assertions characteristic of his metaphysics as the most general assertions pertaining to everything that exists.

As is clear from the above characterisation of ontology this

77

discipline attempts to explain the conceptual apparatus which is used in philosophy and everyday life. As such it is a useful discipline but it has a rather auxiliary role.

### Examples of concepts analysed by ontology

Among the concepts with which ontology is much pre-occupied is the concept of substance. This term has had different meanings in philosophy but the fundamental one is that which it was given by Aristotle. He describes substance as that of which something can be predicated but which cannot itself be predicated of anything else. In other words, substance is everything to which some properties can be attributed, which can stand in a certain relationship to something else, which can be in this or that state, etc., but which is not itself a property, a relation or a state, etc. Examples of substances are: this chair, this table, this person, in a word concrete individual things and persons. To substance are opposed properties which in contradistinction to substances can be predicated of something, relations which also in contradistinction to substances can obtain between certain objects, states, etc. The scholastics emphasised the self-subsistence of substance in contrast to the non-self-subsistence of properties, relations, states, etc. The property of redness, for example, cannot exist except in a substance that possesses it. This particular rose, however, of which redness is an attribute, does not need any foundations for its existence but exists on its own. This self-subsistence of substance they considered to be its essential property and they defined substance as *res, qui convenit esse in se vel per se*.

Another important metaphysical concept analysed in ontology is that of real being (*esse reale*) as contrasted with merely conceived being (*esse in intellectu*). The Tatra mountains, Niagara Falls, the battle of Leipzig really exist or existed and are examples of what are called 'real beings'. On the other hand, centaurs, Balladyna, the meeting of Zagloba with Burlaj exist or existed only in thought and are examples of what are called 'merely conceived beings'. 'Merely conceived beings' do not exist in the primary sense of the word and existence can be attributed to them only in a figurative sense. When we say that Zeus existed in the thought of the Greeks, we mean to say the Greeks thought about Zeus (or believed in Zeus).

As a third example of concepts analysed by ontology we shall take the concept of real objects and contrast it with the concept of ideal objects. Real objects are objects, events, etc. which existed, exist or will exist in time. Ideal objects are called timeless entities. The most frequently cited examples of ideal objects are numbers, ideal geometrical figures (points, lines, etc.), relations holding among them, etc. Also cited are such abstractions as beauty, justice, virtue, conceived not as properties realised in concrete objects but as properties in abstraction from objects and thus beauty in itself, justice as such, etc.

We have mentioned three examples of concepts analysed by philosophers within the domain of ontology, concepts which have played an important role in other parts of metaphysics. These are different concepts of objects with which different concepts of existence are connected. The sense in which we attribute existence to substance is different from that in which we attribute it to properties, relations, etc; it is different for real objects and merely conceived ones; it is different again when we talk about the existence of real objects as contrasted with the existence of ideal ones. All these different concepts of existence have been analysed by philosophers in the course of the history of ontology. Parallel to the analysis of different concepts of existence connected with the meaning of the different concepts of objects we have just mentioned, philosophers have been concerned with the analysis of such concepts as that of possibility and necessity. These concepts of different modes of being (in Latin *modi existendi*) have been called modal concepts.

The concepts mentioned are examples of only some of the concepts investigated by ontology. Ontology is concerned with the analysis of many others as well. So, for example, ontology analyses the concept of causal relationship, the concept of goal, the concepts of space and spatial relationships, of time and of temporal relationships and many others.

## Ontological assertions

The general assertions of ontology are based, as we have said, on the analyses of these concepts. Among the most celebrated of ontological principles are for example: the ontological principle of contradiction, asserting that no object can possess a certain property and not possess it; the ontological principle of the excluded middle which asserts that every object must either possess a given property or not possess it. These principles, though they seem to be quite obvious, have been hotly disputed.

The principle of contradiction and the principle of excluded middle are also to be found in formal logic. This is also the case with many other ontological assertions. Ontology is concerned with analyses of concepts not sufficiently clarified in order to base a precise theory on them. When the analysis of these concepts is carried out sufficiently its results are taken over by some other science which bases on these analyses a system of assertions having the character of a deductive theory, that is a science having the methodological form characteristic of mathematics. So for instance contemporary formal logic, which is, as regards its method, a science akin to mathematics, includes the theory of classes and the theory of relations. In these two parts formal logic makes assertions which could very well be included in ontology because they are solely based on establishing the meaning of such terms as 'individual object', 'property', 'relation', etc. Indeed some logical authors call this part of formal logic ontology.

In this way ontology becomes a foundation out of which particular sciences grow. On the other hand, some problems of an ontological character emerge out of particular sciences. This happens particularly at the time when these sciences stumble in the course of their development across certain difficulties which have their source in insufficient clarification of some basic concepts used in them. A need then arises for the clarification of these concepts, scientists turn their attention to the realm of ontology and co-operation takes place between specialists and philosophers.

# 8

## Metaphysical inferences from reflections on knowledge

### The problem of ideal objects: the controversy about universals

*Platonic ideas.* The problem mentioned in the title of this section is connected with the dispute between apriorists and empiricists which we encountered when discussing the epistemological problem of the 'source of knowledge'. In this epistemological problem we were concerned with the question which of the two methods, aprioristic or empirical, the method of reasoning or the method of experience, leads to knowledge of reality. Plato was an extreme apriorist because he thought that only knowledge based on reason leads to knowledge of what really exists, and therefore to knowledge of reality, whereas experience acquaints us only with the world of appearances. Rational knowledge is knowledge acquired by means of concepts, experiential knowledge by means of perceptions and images. If only rational cognition acquaints us with true reality then this true reality must be made of entities which can be grasped solely by means of concepts and not by what is given to us in perceptions and imagination. Those entities which can be apprehended in thought only by abstract concepts and which are not accessible to perception and imagination are called by Plato ideas.

What are these objects that are called ideas? According to

Plato, such things are included among them as goodness in itself which, in contrast to particular good people, good deeds, etc. which can be imagined, can be grasped only by thought. Beauty in itself is also an idea because it can be apprehended conceptually in contrast to particular beautiful objects which can be perceived or imagined.

*Universals.* Among ideas are included first of all what are called general objects such as man in general, horse in general, etc., that is universals. Particular people or particular horses can be imagined; man in general or horse in general, on the other hand, are objects that can be grasped only conceptually. In order to make clear what we mean by these general objects, for example what we mean by horse in general, let us consider the two following statements: 'every horse is herbivorous' and 'the horse is common in Europe'. The first of these statements talks about particular horses and describes them as herbivorous animals. The second is not concerned with any particular horse, because we cannot sensibly assert of any particular horse that it is a common animal. This 'commonness' is ascribed to the species of horse and not to particular horses. Now this species of horses, like the species of men and others, are general objects, which Plato includes among ideas.

Since according to Plato only rational cognition acquaints us with true reality and this rational cognition acquaints us only with entities that can be grasped by means of concepts, that is acquaints us with ideas, therefore Plato concludes, only the world of ideas is true reality and the world of individual things accessible to sensory cognition is not true reality.

Plato's doctrine was a challenge to common sense. Because of this it has met with more or less radical opposition in the history of philosophy. The dispute about this topic is known in the history of philosophy as the controversy about universals because the Latin name for general objects is *universalia*. Besides Plato's position, which attributes to universals real and self-subsistent being, there is also Aristotle's view which does not deny existence to universals but does not regard them as self-subsistent, as capable of existence independently of individual things. According to Aristotle universals exist only in individual things, being their essential properties, that is, as Aristotle put it, being the form of individual things. However, according to Aristotle, only individual things have self-subsistent (substantial) being. This kind of being is characteristic of particular people. The idea of man, that is humanity, exists only as the essential property of particular people, not in abstraction from them but in them. Plato's doctrine, which attributes real and self-subsistent being to universals, is called *radical conceptual realism*. Aristotle's doctrine attributing real but not self-subsistent being to them, the kind of being that is grounded in particular objects, is called *moderate conceptual realism*.

*Conceptualism* on the other hand opposes both these forms of conceptual realism; it denies that ideas have real existence at all and attributes to them only conceived being. Universals do not exist, only their concepts do.

*Nominalism* goes even further in its opposition to conceptual realism, and denies both that universals and that concepts exist. According to the nominalist a thought about man in general which is not specific as to sex, age, height or any other characteristic which can distinguish people from one another, such a thought cannot be conceived. According to the nominalist there exist only general terms, there are no general concepts, and, even more so, there are no general objects.

*The contemporary form of the dispute about universals.* The old philosophical controversy about the existence of universals appears in a different form in modern philosophy. The contemporary form of the problem is concerned with the question whether aprioristic disciplines such as mathematics investigate a world that is fully real but quite different from the world given to us in sense experience, a world of ideal entities such as numbers, mathematical functions, etc. which exist independently of our minds, or whether this world does not exist at all. An aspect of this controversy has already been discussed in the chapter devoted to the problem of the source of knowledge and concerned with the character of mathematical axioms. According to some (the phenomenologists) we are not allowed to accept axioms in an arbitrary way; axioms are the expression of knowledge of an ideal world which exists independently of us and is accessible to cognition through the intuition of essences. According to others, mathematical axioms are not the expression of knowledge of certain ideal entities which exist independently of us, but are only a kind of definitions (are implicit definitions) of some terms contained in them and as such can to a great extent be taken in an arbitrary way. This other school does not recognise any world of ideal entities existing independently of our minds and whose cognition is the task of mathematics. According to it there exists only the world of real entities that are accessible to empirical cognition and mathematics merely prepares the conceptual apparatus for the cognitive articulation of this world.

## The problem of metaphysical idealism: (a) Subjective idealism

*The consequences of epistemological idealism.* Epistemological idealism asserts the thesis, with regard to the limits of our knowledge, that our minds are not capable of knowing a reality external to it. This thesis has two versions, depending on what is meant by reality external to our minds, and these correspond to the two forms of epistemological idealism: (i) immanent idealism, which holds that our minds can acquire knowledge only of their own experiences, (ii) transcendental idealism which holds that our minds can know only their own constructions (cf. pp. 50–2). The philosopher who adheres to the position of epistemological idealism must regard everything that our minds know as complexes of some mental states of the knowing subject or as constructions by the knowing subject.

Among the objects which we know belong, first of all, physical nature and in particular bodies. It is to them that the consequences of epistemological idealism we are discussing mainly applies. It follows from epistemological idealism in its immanent version that bodies are certain experiences of the knowing subject. And so Berkeley, for instance, the representative of immanent idealism, considers body and soul, houses, trees, tables, chairs, etc. to be nothing but complexes of impressions of the mind perceiving them. It follows from epistemological idealism in its transcendental version that the bodies which we know are only constructions of our minds.

*The thesis of subjective idealism.* The reduction of bodies to complexes of impressions or their degradation to a certain kind of construction of our minds forces the adherents of this view to ask the question whether the existence attributed to bodies is to be taken in a literal sense or in some figurative sense. Let us examine the answers that are given to this question by the immanent and by the transcendent idealists. For the immanent idealist bodies are no more than impressions or complexes of impressions of the knowing subject. But impressions are not substances which can exist self-subsistently. An impression is an experience of a certain subject and can exist only in relation to a subject. When we say that an impression exists the word 'exists' does not have the further irreducible meaning which it has when we talk about substances. 'An impression exists' means 'someone is having an impression', 'someone experiences it'. Similarly when we say that a complex of impressions exists, it amounts to saying that someone has experienced this complex. Since bodies and thus trees, houses, tables, chairs are only complexes of impressions, their existence reduces to the fact that someone experiences them. We can not assert the existence of bodies in the same irreducible sense that we assert the existence of substances. Bodies are not substances but mental states, impressions or complexes of them. In asserting their existence we attribute it to them only in the sense we do to impressions; therefore 'bodies exist' means: 'someone (a given mental subject) is experiencing them', 'someone is conscious of them'. This is the thesis of subjective metaphysical idealism in its immanent version in relation to bodies. Its most outstanding proponent was Berkeley, who expressed it in a concise formula that, as regards bodies, their *esse* = *percipi*, their existence consists in the fact that they are perceived.

Transcendental idealism does not identify the object of knowledge, and in particular bodies, with certain mental states, it does not identify them therefore with impressions but it puts them on the same level as poetic fictions, as mythological persons, etc. These fictions are not mental states, they are not the thoughts of anyone. (The thoughts of Sienkiewicz existed at the turn of the nineteenth and twentieth centuries but Zagloba, who was created by the thought of Sienkiewicz, did not exist then. The fictitious Zagloba is therefore not identical with any thought of Sienkiewicz. We sometimes say about such fictions that they exist in a certain sense; we say, for instance, that among the Olympian gods there existed the god of thunder but that there did not exist a god of the polar lights. But when we say this we do not take 'existence' in its literal sense because we know that the god of thunder, i.e. Zeus, did not exist in the literal sense, any more than the god of the polar lights existed.

We mean that Zeus existed but only in the beliefs of the Greeks and this means only that the Greeks believed that Zeus existed. The word 'exists' in reference to poetic fictions, mythical persons, etc. means: someone thought about them, someone believed in them, etc.)

The transcendental idealist puts bodies on the same level as such fictions, such constructions of thought, when he thinks that our minds cannot know anything but their own constructions. Hence it follows that when we ascribe 'existence' to bodies we do not take this 'existence' literally but that it means here: 'someone thinks about bodies in a particular way', 'someone is somehow aware of these bodies'. It is not indifferent in which way we are aware of these bodies but this is further examined by transcendental idealists. We shall discuss it later.

*Subjective metaphysical idealism does not therefore recognise nature, and in particular bodies, as something that exists in a literal and not further reducible sense of the word, but contends that the 'existence' of bodies has a different sense, so that in ascribing 'existence' to them we do so legitimately in so far as what we say can be reduced to an assertion that a given mental subject behaves in a certain way, that it experiences certain impressions, that it thinks about these bodies in a certain way, etc.*

This is the basic thesis of subjective metaphysical idealism. It is often expressed differently. It is said that according to subjective idealism bodies do not exist independently of the knowing subject but that they possess a being that is dependent on the subject. Berkeley's thesis *esse = percipi* is sometimes formulated as that bodies exist only on the condition that someone perceives them or even that they exist only when they are perceived by someone. But this formulation distorts the sense of the idealistic doctrine. According to it bodies do not exist in a literal sense even when they are being perceived. Nor is the thesis concerned with whether their perception by a subject is a condition of their existence in a literal sense. The perception of a body does not (according to the idealists) make it something that exists in a literal sense since to bodies conceived as complexes of impressions we cannot ascribe existence in the literal sense in which we talk about the existence of substances.

*Reality and its appearance in the light of subjective idealism.* It has been argued against the idealists that their position blurs the difference between physical reality and its appearances. A man who does not philosophise says that if he perceives a real table he does experience some impressions but in addition there is a genuine table in front of him which exists in a literal sense. When I undergo a hallucination and it only appears to me that I perceive a table then, in actual fact, I do have the same impressions as before, but no table really exists (in a literal sense) in front of me. For the idealist, on the other hand, a table never exists in a literal sense; if we assert that a table does exist we take this term in a figurative sense in which the statement 'a table exists' means 'someone has impressions with which the word "table" is associated'. The idealist therefore is unable to distinguish the perception of a real table from a hallucination of it in the way that is usually done. For the idealist there is no difference between physical reality and the hallucination of it.

This objection was taken account of by the idealists and they tried to parry it. Thus idealists do draw a distinction between an appearance and a real body. Although the real body is, according to immanent idealists, the same kind of complex of someone's impressions as is the appearance of a body, the real body is a complex of impressions in a special way. Berkeley, who was a bishop, accepts that an omniscient God constantly perceives the entire material universe. But this material universe is nothing other than the totality of impressions that God experiences: the existence of the material universe is to consist in the fact that it is perceived by God. Man can have impressions which correspond to the impressions of God but he can also have different impressions. The former of these, or complexes of them, are physical bodies, the latter are only the appearance of bodies. Real bodies are then for Berkeley special complexes of impressions in that they are identical with the complexes of impressions experienced by God.

By an appeal to the divine omniscience which maintains the universe in existence, Berkeley also prevents other objections to idealism from arising. Thus if nature is identified with impressions experienced by people it has to be admitted that nature did not exist before the appearance of men. It has to be admitted that the inside of a room comes into existence and disappears when he ceases to look at it. These consequences are avoided by Berkeley because for him the material world is the totality of impressions experienced by God, who according to religion, is eternal and omniscient.

It should be mentioned that Berkeley also gives another account of the difference between real bodies and their appearances. Material reality consists only of those complexes of impressions whose arrangement exhibits a certain continuity and regularity. Dreams and illusions are distinct from reality in being capricious and irregular.

As regards transcendental idealism its chief proponent, Kant, distinctly opposes the appearances of reality, that is fictions, to phenomena, to which he ascribes empirical reality (cf. pp. 59–61). According to transcendental idealism the material world is only a construction of our minds, of the same kind as poetic fictions. In a literal sense it does not exist, on a par with fictions. Both the material world and fictions 'exist' merely in a figurative sense, namely in the sense that someone thinks about them in a certain way. The difference between the 'existence' of the material world which is empirical reality, and the 'existence' of fictions and illusions consists in the fact that thoughts about the material world, about empirical reality, satisfy certain conditions which are not satisfied by thoughts about fictions. The material world is described in judgements satisfying the criteria of the experimental method, thoughts about fictions do not satisfy these criteria. The difference between the material world and the world of fiction thus consists, according to transcendental idealism, in the fact that the criterion of experience supports the material world and does not support, indeed it contradicts, fictions. Everyone who is not an idealist will surely accept this assertion. In the fact that the criterion of experience supports the material world non-idealists see an argument in favour of the existence of the material world in a literal sense, that is independently of our minds. The idealist on the other hand rejects this inference. For him the criterion of experience does not lead to judgements asserting what really is, what exists in a literal sense, what is a thing in itself, but leads only to judgements describing certain constructions of our minds, only certain intentional objects. This is the way in which transcendental idealists, without giving up their basic thesis which asserts that the whole material reality is a construction of our minds, nevertheless make the distinction within the realm of these constructions between the material world, which is 'empirical reality', and the world of fictions and illusions.

## (b) Objective idealism

*The inadequacies of subjective idealism.* Transcendental idealism does not stop in its development at the level of subjective idealism. Subjective idealism (in its transcendental version) recognises bodies and the whole of material nature to be constructions of our minds which do not exist in a literal sense, that is which are not things in themselves; souls and the whole mental world on the other hand it recognises as fully real, it ascribes existence in a literal sense to them, recognises them as 'things in themselves'. This position is not compatible with the basic tenets of transcendental idealism. As we have already said in the chapter devoted to epistemological idealism, it degrades the material world given to us in experience to the level of constructions of our minds and deprives it of its character as a reality independent of our minds. This is because its analysis of the method of experience leads it to the conclusion that this method cannot go beyond the constructions of our minds, cannot reach to things in themselves.

But it is not only knowledge of the material world that we obtain from experience. The mental world is also known through experience. We distinguish, in addition to external experience in which the material world is given, also inner experience in which we know the mental world. If the analysis of experience in general shows that it is not capable of reaching beyond the constructions of our minds to things in themselves, then it follows that, not only bodies and the whole material world, but also souls and the whole mental world are only constructions of our minds, are only intentional objects, and not things in themselves.

This consequence entailed by transcendental idealism is drawn by a metaphysical trend called *objective idealism*. It is called objective idealism and opposed to subjective idealism because the latter considers the world given to us in experience to be a construction of our minds, a correlate of the individual consciousness of man, that is of the soul, whereas objective idealism considers the world given to us in experience, both the material world and the mental world, thus the whole material and spiritual reality, to be a correlate of an entity which is called the *objective spirit*. We shall attempt to present this difficult and entangled doctrine in a clear and accessible way, as far as possible.

*Judgements in the psychological sense and judgements in the logical sense.* Let us remind ourselves that transcendental subjective idealism considers nature to be a collection of merely *intentional* objects (constructions of our minds) which are described in judgements satisfying the criteria of truth and in particular the criterion of experience. Even if we abstract from the basic objection which arises when nature is treated as only a construction of our minds and not as something that really exists, that is in a literal sense, the above doctrine requires certain modifications and corrections even for the idealist himself.

The question arises whether nature is a totality of intentional objects described in judgements satisfying the criterion of truth but only those that were asserted by people or whether judgements asserted by no-one describe this totality as well. If we agree that we are concerned only with judgements actually asserted by someone then the reality described by them would be very fragmentary and full of gaps. The point is that actual human knowledge is limited and it would be paradoxical to assert that nature is exhausted by what people know of it. We should therefore favour rather the second possibility and interpret the thesis of transcendental idealism to mean that nature is the totality of intentional objects described by judgements satisfying the criterion of truth (and in particular the criterion of experience), both judgements which were asserted by someone and those no-one asserted.

If we accept the second interpretation we come upon another difficulty. What are these judgements that are asserted by no-one? Judgements are mental phenomena and mental phenomena always occur in someone's consciousness. If a judgement is a mental phenomenon then it would have to be asserted by someone at some time. This difficulty exists however only if we mean by 'judgement' a certain kind of mental phenomenon. However, the word 'judgement' is not used only to denote certain mental phenomena. When we talk about judgements in logic we do not mean any mental phenomena. We say that the judgement $2 \times 2 = 4$ is one judgement and the judgement $3 \times 3 = 9$ is another, different from the first. When we say this the term 'the judgement: $2 \times 2 = 4$' does not refer to any mental experience or anyone else's, experiences which I or another would express with the sentence '$2 \times 2 = 4$', but we are referring to the meaning of the sentence '$2 \times 2 = 4$' which is a single thing. This single meaning of the sentence '$2 \times 2 = 4$' is neither my conception nor anyone else's, it is no-one's mental experience, but is, as it were, the common content of all these thoughts which are expressed by the sentence '$2 \times 2 = 4$'. This single content can, so to speak, be embodied in many thoughts which can differ among themselves in many respects (for example, as regards clarity, etc.) but agree with each other as regards their content.

*The world of objective spirit.* In the conception of judgement sketched above which is used in logic, as opposed to the conception of judgement used in psychology, we find a way out of the difficulties of the concept of a judgement not asserted by anyone. These judgements in the logical sense, these meanings of sentences, are not mental phenomena, do not have to be related to any mental subject. We can talk about judgements (in the logical sense) which have been asserted by someone and about those which have been asserted by no-one. Those that were asserted by someone happened to be those that became the content of someone's thoughts; those which were asserted by no-one are those which did not occur to anybody.

Where are we to look for these 'judgements in the logical sense', these judgements not asserted by anyone? They are not to be found in the mental world, and not in the material world either. Those who recognise such judgements place them in the world of Platonic ideas, in the world of ideal, timeless entities, in which, according to Platonising thinkers, numbers and other abstract entities such as general objects (universals) are to be found and to which these 'judgements in the logical sense' show a certain similarity. Like general objects (such as horse in general) they are something that remains one and the same, indivisible, although embodied in different individual thoughts of which they are the common content. As entities belonging to the world of Platonic ideas these 'judgements in the logical sense' are called ideal judgements. Apart from ideal judgements we can find in this world ideal concepts which are the ideal meanings of terms in the same sort of way as judgements are the ideal meaning of sentences. Those ideal judgements, ideal concepts etc. are the part of the Platonic world of ideas known as the world of logical entities or the *world of spirit* which, for the sake of sharper contrast with the mental world, is called the *world of objective spirit*. The mental world comprises mental phenomena such as judgements, concepts (in the psychological sense of these words) which are always experienced by a subject or asserted by it and therefore are something subjective. The world of spirit comprises judgement and concepts, in the logical sense of these words, and thus judgements and concepts which do not belong to any subject, are not subjective.

*The thesis of objective idealism.* Now after these distinctions and corrections what is the thesis of objective idealism? It goes as follows: *nature is the totality of merely intentional objects asserted in ideal judgements which satisfy the criterion of truth.* As merely intentional objects they do not possess, according to this thesis, full reality, existence, in a literal sense, cannot be ascribed to them. *The attribution of existence to the objects of nature has only a figurative sense and means only that these objects are asserted in ideal judgements (quite regardless of whether they are known to anyone or to no-one) which satisfy the criterion of truth.*

This is the basic content of the thesis of objective idealism.

The analogous thesis of subjective idealism according to which the objects of nature exist only in the sense that someone (a given mental subject) asserts them in judgements satisfying the criterion of experience was summarised by the adherents of this idealism by saying that the objects of nature are merely phenomena present to a given mental subject. If we proceed analogously we can express the thesis of objective idealism in the following summary way: the objects of nature are merely phenomena present to the objective spirit.

Objective idealism considers both the objects of the material world and the objects of the mental world, including mental subjects, that is souls, as phenomena present to the objective spirit. Human souls are not things in themselves for objective idealism, they are not something that exists in a literal sense but something that exists only in a figurative sense. In this way objective idealism degrades the whole of nature, both physical and mental, to the level of phenomena.

The only true reality, the only sphere of beings which exist in a literal and not a figurative sense, is considered by objective idealism to be the world of objective spirit and thus the world of Platonic ideas. Nature is only a correlate of this world, is only its phenomenon. Objective idealism thus closely appropriates to Platonic idealism.

*Representatives of objective idealism.* We have thus presented the basic thoughts of objective idealism. This presentation is rather remote from the texts in which its adherents express their thoughts. In the whole of philosophy there are no more confusing and difficult arguments than those we can find in works propounding the doctrine of objective idealism. This doctrine is a development of some thoughts contained in Kant's transcendental idealism. In our presentation of this doctrine we attempted to show it as such a development: in his own arguments Kant hesitated between subjective and objective idealism. It was only Kant's followers and above all the trinity of nineteenth-century German idealism, Fichte, Schelling and Hegel, who decisively adopted the position of objective idealism but they presented it in a most confusing form, full of hypostases. In the nineteenth century and at the beginning of the twentieth, objective idealism was also represented by the Marburg and Baden schools of neo-Kantians (Cohen, Natorp, Windelband, Rickert) whose arguments are a little more digestible than those of their predecessors.

*Hegel's dialectic.* Among objective idealists and in particular by Hegel the following idea is emphasised: if nature is merely a phenomenon of the world of objective spirit, then the laws governing nature are only a reflection of the laws governing the world of objective spirit. But in the world of objective spirit and therefore in the world of logical entities, the laws of logic rule. Consequently the laws of logic must be reflected in the laws of nature.

Hegel called the laws of logic which rule in the world of logical entities the laws of dialectics. They are supposed to be laws which establish a certain hierarchy among (ideal) concepts, starting from the most general of them, the concept of being. The principle of this hierarchy is that the concepts in question form contradictory pairs, for example being and non-being, which are called by Hegel thesis and antithesis. After each such pair in this hierarchy comes a third concept, which Hegel calls the synthesis, and which contains in itself elements taken from both the thesis and the antithesis. So, for instance, the synthesis of the concepts of being and non-being, is, according to Hegel, the concept of becoming, because what is becoming already is and yet in a sense is not. This 'dialectical' hierarchy of ideal concepts has, according to Hegel, its equivalents in the chronological order in which the objects of nature appear one after another. In nature each state of being, according to Hegel, is accompanied by its antithesis. This thesis and antithesis struggling with each other give rise to a new state, this being a certain synthesis of the struggling opposites. This is, according to Hegel, how the laws of dialectics govern the course of nature. However, Hegel does not consider the dialectical laws governing the course of nature as something primitive which is to be established empirically. On the contrary, he considers the dialectics of nature to be the consequence of the fact that nature is only a reflection of the world of spirit in which dialectical order reigns and which must correspondingly prevail in nature.

*The dialectic of Hegel and the dialectic of Marx.* Hegel's dialectic is supposed to contain the most general laws governing all development, all change occurring in nature. Hegel arrives at these laws in a purely speculative manner, *a priori* and without recourse to experience. One of the assumptions on which Hegel relies is his idealism. However the conclusions drawn from certain assumptions can be true in spite of the fact that the assumptions from which they are drawn are false. It is thus possible to reject Hegel's idealism entirely but nevertheless accept that nature is ruled by the laws of dialectics.

This is precisely the procedure followed by Karl Marx who knew Hegel's teaching well. In agreement with Hegel, Marx asserted that processes of development and all change occur in nature in accordance with the laws of dialectics, but at the same time he rejected the whole aprioristic basis on which Hegel rested his dialectic. Rejecting Hegel's aprioristic arguments, Marx accepts the laws of dialectic because, in his view, experience supports these laws. Marx was a materialist, that is to say he considered physical nature to be the truest of true realities, he denied existence both to souls and to the objective spirit and thus to what, according to idealists, whether subjective or objective, was supposed to constitute true reality. Marx was also a radical empiricist, that is he did not recognise any other way of justifying assertions than experience. Rejecting both Hegel's aprioristic method of justifying the laws of dialectics and the idealistic foundations on which Hegel rests it and finding, on the other hand, an empirical justification (as he supposed) for the laws of dialectics and linking it to materialism, Marx, as he put it, turned dialectics upside down. Connecting dialectics with materialism in this way, Marx became the main creator of a philosophical trend called dialectic materialism of which we shall speak in the next chapter.

### (c) Metaphysical realism

*Naive and critical realism.* The position opposed to meta-physical idealism is called *metaphysical realism.* Its basic thesis asserts that *bodies exist in a literal sense.* Realism is a natural view to which everyone adheres before epistemological reflection. This natural realism, when untouched by any reflection on knowledge, is called *naive realism.*

In addition to this kind of realism we can also distinguish *critical realism* which, after epistemological reflection and consideration of idealistic arguments, comes to reject them and to support the thesis about the existence of natural objects in a literal sense; these objects are identified neither with complexes of impressions nor with constructions of our minds but are recognised as trans-subjective beings. Critical realism attacks, first of all, the arguments of epistemological idealism which, as we have already seen, are the main foundation of metaphysical idealism. In reflecting upon the process of the perception of bodies critical realism often finds that ordinary sensory experience gives us a picture of the world that is not wholly free from subjective constituents and it attempts to rectify this picture and to free it from these subjective constituents. By and large critical realists think that the picture of the world which is given immediately to our senses does not correspond to reality. In the real material world there are no colours, sounds and scents such as our senses present to us. The colours, sounds, scents, etc. perceived by us are only the subjective reactions of our psychophysical organisation to certain stimuli coming from the external world. All these qualities, which are produced by the organisation of our cognitive faculties and erroneously attributed to objects are called secondary qualities by critical realists and are opposed to primary qualities which are really attributes of bodies. According to critical realists, it is not the picture of the world thrust on our senses that is true but the one which physics presents to us as the result of painstaking inquiries. In accordance with the views affirmed in a given epoch by physics the critical realists recognise this or that picture as giving the true nature of the material world. In the nineteenth century this picture was composed of colourless atoms, possessing, however, a certain shape and size as well as mass and velocity. At the present time this picture is losing its pictorial quality and is becoming rather more a mathematical schema than a model which can be visualised.

The controversy between realism and idealism has been going on for centuries. At the present time we can find serious thinkers representative of both trends. There are very many ambiguities in the problem itself, very many misunderstandings between the disputants; because of this the problem itself should be more exactly stated before one takes a position in this controversy. The present writer has attempted to do this in other works. Deeper penetration into the problem would be outside the scope of this book which is only a review of philosophical problems. In his other works the author has been led to decisive opposition to idealism in all its forms and to giving his unqualified support to the realist position.

# 9

## Metaphysical problems arising from the investigation of nature

### The problem of the substance and structure of the world

At the dawn of European thought in ancient Greece, meta-physical inquiries were devoted to the investigation of nature. The first metaphysicians were in fact called 'the physicists' or, as we should put it today, 'the naturalists'. Those first naturalists were interested in very general problems and arrived at solutions to them in a purely speculative way, without painstaking and detailed observation and investigation of facts. Among these were, above all, two problems: the problem of the raw material of nature, that is the problem of the substance nature is made of, and, secondly, the problem of the general structure of nature. Both these problems, which already occupied the centre of interest in Greek philosophy, run through the entire course of philosophy and are at the heart of the problems of metaphysics.

Investigating the question of what substances nature is made of, the first philosophers had in mind corporeal nature. With further philosophical development the attention of philosophers was turned both to the corporeal nature given to us in external (sensory) experience and to the mental nature which is given to us in inner experience. In modern philosophy the problem of substance takes the form of the question whether there exist both mental and corporeal substances or whether only one of these kinds of substance exists. In a word the problem of substance takes the form of the problem of soul and body. The original problems attracting philosophers who aimed at a deeper understanding of what bodies are, what in the last analysis are their ultimate components, are contained today in the philosophy of nature in which physicists have more to say than philosophers.

The problem of the structure of nature occurs in two basic forms in the history of philosophy. One is the problem of determinism and indeterminism and deals with the question whether everything in nature has a cause; the other deals with the problem of teleology and mechanism and considers the question whether the world is arranged purposively or not. Among the problems about the structure of nature we may mention finally the problems of the spatial and temporal structure of the world and to these too physicists rather than philosophers are competent to address themselves.

### The problem of soul and body

*What substances exist in nature?* This problem occupies a central place in the metaphysical investigations of modern philosophy. There are many questions contained in it but the foremost is the question of what kinds of substances exist in nature. The main types of answer to this question appear under the names: dualism, materialism, spiritualism and the identity theory, that is monism proper.

*Dualism.* Dualism is the trend whose main thesis contends that both spiritual and corporal substances exist, that is both souls and bodies. This trend is in harmony with the original view of people brought up within the sphere of Christian culture. According to it, bodies are the basis of physical phenomena; bodies move, change temperature, change in shape, can conduct electricity, etc. but bodies do not think, do not feel, do not suffer and do not experience joy. These latter phenomena, known to us from inner experience, require, because of their essential nature, a quite different basis. This basis is the soul which thinks, feels, rejoices, suffers, etc.

*Extreme and moderate dualism.* Dualism occurs in the history of philosophy in two different forms. In its radical form it is held by Augustine and Descartes. A more moderate form of dualism is adopted by Aristotle and Thomas Aquinas. According to Aristotle, it is bodies that really and self-subsistently exist first of all, that is bodies in the first instance are real substances. In each body, however, Aristotle distinguishes two components: matter and form. The matter of a body is what it is made of, and so its material, its raw stuff. The matter of a clay vase is the clay of which the vase is made. Aristotle calls the form of a body that which makes a thing what it is and not anything else. For instance, the form of a clay vase is that which makes this object a vase and not anything else. In the example of the vase, its shape is its form. However, its shape is not always the form of an object since the shape of an object does not always decide that it is what it is and not anything else. For example, the form of an apple tree is not only its shape but also the other properties which are attributes of the apple tree as a plant, for instance, its capacity to assimilate inorganic nourishment, its capacity for growth, its capacity for reproduction, and many others.

Man too is made of matter and form. His matter is the chemical bodies he is made of. His form, on the other hand, is everything through which all these chemical bodies that are the components of man are made into a living being, who feels and thinks and is not merely a dead, insensitive and thoughtless mass of flesh and bones. Man's form is thus everything that makes man a living organism in general and thus what man shares with plants which are also alive, furthermore everything man shares with animals, for example feeling, the capacity of moving from place to place, etc., and finally those characteristics which are man's alone and distinguish him from animals. This last, according to Aristotle, is the capacity for thinking, that is reason. Now the human form made of these various components Aristotle called the human soul. Man is an animated body composed of matter and soul. Man's body, therefore, is identical with matter. Matter is what we can distinguish in an abstract way in an animated human body. Similarly the soul is only an abstract component of the body. The body and the soul are therefore not entities having the same kind of existence. The body is a substance capable of self-subsistent existence and does not require any further basis for its realisation. The soul, on the other hand, as a form, that is as a complex of essential human attributes, exists only in the way attributes exist, that is in relation to a body; the existence of the soul consists in its being attributed to a body.

Within the doctrine of Aristotle, who, in opposition to Plato, denied that form can exist without matter, the admission of the existence of the soul in abstraction from the body, and thus the admission of the existence of the soul after man's death, was a kind of inconsistency. How could the form, that is to say an essential attribute, exist without that of which it is an attribute? In spite of this, Aristotle accepted immortality and he asserted that only the reasoning part of the human soul does not perish with the death of the body. This thesis about the immortality of individual souls was attacked by the medieval Arab philosopher Averroes. Because of this, Thomas Aquinas, who in principle accepts Aristotle's doctrine, had to introduce some modifications in order to maintain it while still preserving Aristotle's conception of the soul as the form of man.

The radical version of dualism which we find in Augustine

and Descartes treats souls and bodies as of equal rank, recognising both as self-subsistent beings, as substances which can be the basis for properties without requiring any further basis for their own existence. This radical version of dualism encounters a difficulty when we consider what the relation is between soul and body, how we should conceive a man as a homogeneous entity, although he is made of two different but self-subsistent entities. This form of dualism corresponds to a primitive and very widespread view held in common life.

*Monism and its varieties.* Various monistic metaphysical doctrines arise out of the criticism of this common dualism, doctrines that accept only one kind of substance (one = *monos*) among them materialism, spiritualism and the theory of identity.

*Materialism.* The thesis of materialism in its classical formulation asserts: *only material substances exist*, that is to say: *only bodies are substances*. Spiritual substances, according to materialists, are merely an illusion. There are several varieties of materialism.

*Mechanical materialism* not only denies that spiritual substances exist, it also considers even mental phenomena (thoughts, feelings, etc.) to be physical processes; it most often identifies them with certain physiological processes taking place in the brain or even considers them to be bodies secreted by the brain. (The brain secretes thoughts in the way the liver secretes bile.) Among other representatives of materialism were the French eighteenth-century philosopher Cabanis and the German nineteenth-century philosophers Vogt, Büchner and others.

*Dialectical materialism.* Other versions of materialism do not identify mental phenomena with physiological processes of the brain but recognise certain peculiarities in mental phenomena. However, they consider that the body, and not some other spiritual substance different from the body, is the basis on which mental phenomena occur. What experiences enjoyment and sadness, what thinks and considers, etc. is the body of man and not a soul different from it. This is the position developed by *dialectical materialism* which was created by Engels and Marx. Dialectical materialism considers that matter, in the course of its historical development, has changed its form, being enriched in the course of time in some of its parts by certain new qualities that are irreducible to the qualities it originally possessed. The original dead matter, in which only physico-chemical processes took place, suddenly gained, in certain parts where these processes reached a high level of complexity, a new quality, irreducible to physico-chemical qualities – the quality we call life. In this way the first organisms were originated. In the further course of development of living matter, when physico-chemical and biological processes taking place in it achieve a sufficiently high level of evolution, a new quality again appeared in it. Matter has acquired consciousness; mental life has been born in it. Mental life, however, is not reducible, either to physico-chemical processes, or to biological ones; it is something quite different from these processes, although it is dependent on and conditioned by them. This attainment by matter in the course of its development of ever new qualities which are not reducible to any combination of qualities already possessed takes place, according to dialectical materialists, in one sudden leap and not through gradual evolution.

The form of materialism presented above is called dialectical materialism because its creators combined materialism with dialectics in it. As we have already mentioned when discussing the philosophy of Hegel, Karl Marx, the creator of dialectical materialism, thought that experience confirms the view that nature is governed by the laws of dialectics which Hegel arrived at in a purely speculative manner. This prompted Marx to adopt a dialectical point of view in the investigation of nature and the social life of human beings. This dialectical point of view demands that we should consider nature in its process of becoming and development; as opposed to the 'metaphysical' point of view which considers nature statically, as something fixed and unchangeable. (Dialectical materialists use the terms 'metaphysics' and 'metaphysical' in a different way from that in which they are usually employed.) It demands further that when investigating particular phenomena we should not isolate them from other phenomena but should consider all the possible relations in which the phenomenon being investigated has to others, and in particular its causal relations. This way of investigating nature leads, according to dialectical materialists, to the assertion that it is governed by certain laws which they call the laws of dialectics. Among the four laws of dialectic that are usually mentioned, the most important are: the law of the transformation of quantitative changes into qualitative ones, and the law of the unity and conflict of opposites.

The law of the transformation of quantity into quality affirms that the developmental processes occurring in nature (including the world of human societies) happen in the following way: quantitative changes, that is to say changes during which only the intensity of the measurable characteristics of an object undergo change (as for example its temperature, weight, length, while its non-measurable qualities such as hardness and sex remain the same), after they have achieved a sufficiently high level are transformed suddenly (in a leap) into qualitative changes (that is in which measurable qualities do not change any more but in which a certain non-measurable quality is replaced by another). An example of the transformation of quantity into quality is the freezing of water. Water at the temperature, say, of 20 degrees centigrade, as the result of loss of heat, loses its temperature only gradually, that is it undergoes only quantitative changes. However, at the moment when the cooling water reaches the temperature of 0 degrees centigrade the further loss of heat does not cause any further fall in temperature, instead of this merely quantitative change there occurs a qualitative one, a change from the liquid to the solid state. In the formulation of this law, it is emphasised that this transformation from quantitative into qualitative change occurs suddenly and not gradually. These qualitative changes are called 'dialectical leaps'. Dialectics emphasise that in the process of the becoming of nature large and important changes, which the qualitative changes are, take place by leaps in a revolutionary and not evolutionary fashion. It is also in a revolutionary and not an evolutionary way that great qualitative changes occur in the structure of human societies, although the preparation of these qualitative revolutionary changes is a long drawn out process of quantitative change which occurs in a gradual, evolutionary way.

The second of the laws of dialectics mentioned above, the law of the unity and conflict of opposites, is concerned with the dynamism of developmental processes in nature (and in the world of human society). It affirms that in every process of becoming there always co-exist forces that are struggling with each other. To each of these forces there corresponds a state which is itself opposed to a state to which a second force corresponds. In this way in every phase of the process of becoming there co-exist opposing states which, as it were, struggle against each other. From the struggle of these opposites a certain new state emerges, different from both of the struggling opposites. But even this new state does not last permanently. The forces which uphold it arouse opposing forces; a new struggle of opposites takes place and so on ad infinitum. The law of the unity and conflict of opposites corresponds to Hegel's law of three stages: thesis, antithesis and synthesis. For example, let us consider a body which is in a state of rest and on which a force begins to act. Under the influence of this force the body begins to accelerate, its speed originally equal to zero, gradually increases. As the result of its speed friction and air resistance arise which counteract the force causing the movement. This struggle of the force causing the movement and the frictions that attempt to stop it leads in the end, when force and friction become equal, to the transformation of movement, which was at first accelerated, into a steady movement. From the struggle of these forces, of which one corresponds to accelerated movement and the other to rest, emerges, as if it were their synthesis, a steady movement.

In this law, apart from the correct observation that in every process of becoming there is a struggle of opposing forces, there is also contained the view that in each such process there co-exist opposing and even contradictory states. Because of this the adherents of dialectics set themselves in opposition to certain laws of formal logic, in particular the law of contradiction. The adherents of dialectical materialism think that every change, and thus motion too, implies contradiction. To justify this opinion they refer among other things to the arguments of the ancient school of Eleatic philosophers who tried to show that change and motion are impossible because the very supposition that something moves leads to its own denial and therefore to contradiction. Thus one of these philosophers, Zeno of Elea, argued in the following way: if an arrow released from a bow were moving, then, at every moment of its flight, it would be at a certain definite spot and thus, at every moment of its flight, it would be at rest in that place. And if at every moment of its flight it was at rest, then throughout the whole of its flight it would not move. The supposition, then, that an arrow released from a bow moves leads to its own denial and therefore to a contradiction. This reasoning inclined Eleatic philosophers to think that motion does not really exist. Because the evidence of the senses supports the claim that motion does exist, the Eleatics drew the conclusion that the senses deceive us and that experience is not a trustworthy source of knowledge. This was the path that led from the Eleatics to the extreme apriorism followed by Plato and other ancient philosophers. The dialectical materialists, on the other hand, are empiricists and consider experience to be the ultimate criterion of truth. They draw a different conclusion from Zeno's arguments. Agreeing with Zeno that motion implies contradiction (that is, that the supposition that something moves leads to a contradiction), they do not accept the conclusion drawn by Zeno that motion, as contradictory in itself, does not exist. As empiricists the dialectical materialists recognise the reality of motion because experience unequivocally supports it. They thus assert both that motion exists and that it implies a contradiction. This leads them to the conclusion that contradiction exists and that the law of contradiction, being one of the fundamental canons of formal logic, ruling out all contradiction, is false.*

The representatives of dialectical materialism in formulating their opinions avoid the scholastic term 'substance' and do not assert their materialistic thesis in the words 'only corporeal substances exist'. They prefer to give their materialism the form of the assertion that matter is prior to soul. This means, to start with, that matter existed before spirit (that is, before mental life), which emerged only later in a far advanced stage of the development of matter, and that there-

---

* We shall not go into the discussion of Zeno's argument. For those interested in the matter, I refer to my article 'Zmiznai Sprzecznose' ['Change and Contradiction'], *Mysl Wspolczesna*, VIII-IX (1948) 35-52.

fore genetically matter does not originate from spirit but that spirit originates from matter. Emphasising the chronological and genetic priority of matter to spirit, dialectical materialists think that this is the opinion supported by the results of the investigations of natural science whereas the opposite opinion ascribing the priority to spirit is based on religious beliefs which accept the creation of the world by God who stands outside the material world.

But the materialists oppose not only those who, accepting bodies to be fully real objects, consider them to be the creations of the divine spirit and therefore to be dependent on spirit in the way that an effect depends on its cause or a product on its producer. Maintaining matter's independence of spirit, materialists also deny the form of dependence of matter on spirit that is envisaged by idealists who, depriving matter of full reality, take it to be a kind of fiction, a merely intentional object whose existence consists in the fact that someone thinks about it in a certain way.

*Materialism in conflict with idealism.* Materialism therefore fights its battle on two fronts. First, it fights against idealism of all varieties and thus both subjective idealism, which takes matter to be a complex of impressions or only a construction of the knowing mind, and objective idealism, which considers the whole of nature, both material and mental, to be only the correlate of the world of logical entities, that is of the objective spirit. Materialists stand firmly on the realistic position and they often put the realistic thesis in the forefront of their doctrine, presenting it as its basic content. In doing so they are incorrect because the realist position does not necessarily imply the materialistic thesis as its consequence. Realism, attributing full reality to nature, need not attribute it only to corporeal nature but can attribute it to mental substances, that is spirits. Realism is compatible with both materialism and dualism.

It is in relation to realism that materialism conducts the second front of its battle in which its opponent is dualism, which also upholds the realistic position.

*Materialism in conflict with dualism.* The controversy between materialism and dualism is a dispute about the existence of souls, conceived as substances of equal status to bodies but different from bodies. The proper opponent to materialism is then radical dualism as represented by Augustine or Descartes. Between moderate dualism represented by Aristotle and moderate materialism represented by dialectical materialists, for example, the contrast is less striking.

In the history of philosophy materialists have been on the attacking side whereas dualists have defended the position that prevailed before the controversy broke out. The materialists' attack consisted, first of all, in showing that acceptance of the existence of the soul, conceived as a thinking substance (or in general as conscious) and different from the body, is devoid of any rational basis. What could the basis be, materialists ask, which would justify in a rational way any existential thesis, that is any thesis asserting that such-and-such a thing really exists? It is only on the basis of experience that we can assert the existence, and particularly the real existence, of anything. It is through experience, direct or indirect, that we are entitled to accept the existence of anything. Experience entitles us to assert the existence of something directly when we see it, feel it, hear it or in general perceive it, indirectly when it is not perceived as a matter of fact but when its existence follows from certain facts that are directly perceived or when its existence must be accepted in order to explain certain observed facts.

Now, materialists argue, neither direct nor indirect experience supports the existence of the soul, if by the soul we mean a thinking substance different from the body. Direct experience does not support it for no-one has ever been, felt, heard or in general perceived it. Indirect experience does not support it either, for the existence of the soul does not follow from any facts of experience nor is the hypothesis assuming the existence of the soul required for the explanation of facts discovered by direct observation. Because of this the doctrine that asserts the existence of thinking substances which are quite different from the body is quite baseless. This doctrine is, as materialists say, a remnant of the primitive phase of the human mind in which whenever any peculiar phenomena were observed in relation to some object a certain substance was postulated which was supposed by its action to cause them. The phenomena of heat prompted primitive naturalist thinkers to assume that the bodies in which these phenomena appear contain in themselves a peculiar substance, different from these bodies, which was called the heat-fluid; electrical phenomena were imputed to some electric substance which was supposed to cause them. Biological phenomena were considered to be the manifestation of the activity of a substance which was called *anima vegetativa* or *spiritus animalis*. Now the way in which the hypothesis of the soul is arrived at is very similar. It is observed that certain bodies are equipped with mental life and it is inferred that this is sufficient reason to assume that a psychic fluid dwells in these bodies and is different from them, which is called the soul.

Contemporary science has broken away from this kind of thinking. The mere fact of the appearance of electrical phenomena in certain bodies is not sufficient reason today for accepting that some substance, which is called electricity, dwells in these bodies. We do, as a matter of fact, accept today that electrons, which are only electric charges and are not burdened with any matter, exist, but their existence is accepted because certain phenomena have been observed (e.g. cathode radiation) whose cause is such that in order to explain it we must accept the hypothesis of the existence of electrons. But we do not believe in the existence of heat-fluid or in the existence of magnetic fluid because no-one has ever perceived them and because we do not find phenomena in experience whose explanation would require the acceptance of the hypothesis of their existence.

To this materialist attack the defenders of the soul reply that the soul has not been seen, felt, heard or in any way sensorily perceived by anyone, but that sense-perception is not the only kind of immediate experience. Apart from sensory experience there is inner experience which assures me that I think, desire, am happy or sad. From this experience I derive the certainty that there exists a thinking, desiring entity and thus a spiritual and not a corporeal entity. The verdict of inner experience, in fact, is far more certain than the verdict of the senses. The existence of the bodies which I accept on the basis of the verdict of the senses can be doubted because against this verdict the objection can be raised that it all may have been a dream, that my senses might be deluding me and that the entire sensory world is only a mirage. But such an objection cannot in the least diminish the certainty of inner experience when it informs me that I think, perceive and therefore that I exist as a thinking entity. Let us assume that I err in believing in the world of bodies; that I err in many other matters. Now in order to err there must exist a thinking entity because to err means to think falsely. The existence of the soul, therefore, its defenders argue, is much better grounded in the evidence of experience than the existence of bodies.

This defence of the soul does not undermine the materialists' convictions. They ask what is it that this inner experience informs me about? About the fact that I think, desire, am happy or sad, etc. It informs me that certain phenomena of thinking, desiring, enjoying or suffering, that is certain mental phenomena, occur in me. It informs me that I exist as a thinking, desiring, etc. entity. No materialist denies this. But does it follow from the existence of thinking entities that there exist spiritual entities, that is souls? The answer to this question will depend on the definition of the term 'soul'. If 'soul' means only 'thinking entity' then of course inner experience does inform us that the soul exists. If, however, 'soul' is to mean 'thinking entity different from the body' then from the fact that there are thinking entities it does not follow that there exist souls different from bodies. In order to prove the existence of souls conceived as thinking substances and different from bodies, it is not sufficient to demonstrate that thinking substances exist but it must be shown also that they are not bodies, it must be shown that it is not the body that thinks, desires, is happy or sad.

However, materialists assert, there are good reasons for thinking quite the opposite. It is known from daily life and particularly from the observation of pathological states how much mental phenomena depend on our bodies. Damage to the brain leads to the disappearance of whole realms of mental life. Surgical operations on the brain cause an entire change in a man's personality; our mental life is also temporarily affected by alcohol, caffeine and by the functioning of the endocrine glands, etc. This very close dependence of mental phenomena on the body makes it highly probable that it is just the body, and not a soul distinct from it, that thinks, desires, is happy or sad, etc. If this whole powerful apparatus of arguments showing the dependence of mental life on the body does not prove indubitably that the substratum of mental phenomena is the body, then it must be pointed out that the defenders of the soul cannot appeal to any such arguments for justification of the opposite thesis, so essential to them, that it is not the body but something distinct from it that thinks, desires, etc.

What sort of argument would they need in order to carry conviction? They would have to produce something that has mental life but is not tied to a body and they would have to show it in experience or prove in some other way that something of this sort exists. The existence of electrons was doubted until in cathode radiation we came across something that had electrical properties (which consisted of the bending of cathode rays in the electric field, in the magnetic direction in which negative electric currents bend) and could not be identified with any chemical body. In order to demonstrate directly the existence of thinking entities which are not bodies in outer or inner experience, we should have to come across a soul extricated from a body in a way similar to that in which we come across electricity extricated from matter. In outer, that is sensory, experience only bodies and bodily phenomena can be given. Outer experience, because of its nature, will never reveal to us a soul liberated from a body, in spite of all the attempts made in this direction by spiritists. In order to come across a soul liberated from a body in inner experience, we should have to wait until our own death and this procedure is inaccessible at any rate to people who are alive. There thus remains only an intermediate procedure: a proof of the existence of entities that are thinking but bodiless. It could be a proof that mental life continues after the death of man and thus a proof of the immortality of the soul or a proof of the existence of other thinking and bodiless beings, a proof of the existence of angels, devils, etc. Such proofs have beeen attempted by theologians and philosophers and are attempted by spiritists; so far, according to materialists, no convincing proof of this kind has been found.

Therefore, materialists conclude, the thesis about the existence of souls conceived as thinking entities distinct from bodies still remains, in spite of the appeal to inner experience, a baseless one. As regards thinking beings known from inner experience the fact of the dependence of mental life on the body of man suggests strongly though not decisively that what thinks in us, feels and desires, is our own body.

This reply by the materialists does not, however, satisfy the defenders of the soul. They contend that, in spite of all this, they can show that it is not our body or any other physical organ that thinks, feels and desires, and thus that what thinks is not the body. In the first place the defenders of the soul emphasise that mental processes by their nature are not something to which we can ascribe position in space. It makes no sense to say that my thoughts are, for example, in my head. It would lead to absurd consequences such as that when my head shakes my thoughts shake together with it, that when my head is one metre distant from yours then my thoughts are one metre distant from yours. Whoever ascribes a position in space to thoughts and to mental phenomena in general – and this is done by those who maintain that it is our body that thinks – transforms mental phenomena into physical ones. Location in space is a characteristic feature of physical phenomena; it is peculiar to mental phenomena that they do not occur in space.

To such arguments materialists could reply that they are not disposed to define physical phenomena as phenomena located in space. If, however, someone wants to define physical phenomena in this way he can do so and from the fact that mental phenomena occur in my brain it follows that on this conception of physical phenomena, mental phenomena are a certain kind of physical phenomena. Dialectical materialism, however, will insist that in that case they are phenomena of a peculiar kind different from both all the phenomena described by physics and chemistry and from all the phenomena described by the biological sciences. The assertion itself, that my thoughts occur in my head, does not appear absurd to materialists.

There is also a second argument which the defenders of the soul produce. My soul, they say, is the same as the I who thinks, that is my self. Now I am quite aware that my self is something single and simple, something which is not made of parts. I possess, as the subject of my mental experiences, various characteristics, I am wise or foolish, noble or wicked, firm or unstable, passionate or cold, but I do not possess any parts or fragments. My body, however, is composed of parts. Therefore I, as the subject of my thoughts, am something distinct from my body. Materialists have no difficulty in combating this argument. This argument, according to them, commits a *petitio principii*, because it assumes beforehand that this I who thinks is something different from the body. Only if we make this assumption in advance can we assert that I, as the subject of my thoughts, do not possess parts. Furthermore, the materialist does not have to assert that what thinks is my whole body nor that it is my entire brain. The point is that the body is apparently made of parts which do not themselves contain parts; formerly chemical atoms were considered to be such ultimate parts of bodies; today elementary particles such as electrons and nuclei are considered as the ultimate parts of bodies. It would not be contradictory to the materialist thesis to assume that what thinks in me is some elementary particle of matter which is a component of my body. And then the subject of my thought, although something material, would not possess parts.

This, then, is the second front of the battle of materialism in which its opponent is the dualism that defends substantial souls. What, then, is the course of this dispute? First, the defenders of the soul produce arguments supporting the existence of souls as substances distinct from bodies and materialists refute these arguments and attempt to show that the thesis accepting the existence of souls distinct from bodies is unfounded. It must be remembered, however, that one who shows the unfounded nature of an opponent's thesis has not thereby established his own.

The defenders of the soul, then, do not consider that they have lost their case but continue the dispute further and adopt the method which has been employed with success by materialists, that is, instead of defending their thesis, they attack the thesis of their opponents. They use as the main weapon in this attack the results of recent physical research. In the light of the latest physical theories, claim the opponents of materialism, it is clear that the concept of matter, which has hitherto been so clear, is beginning to lose its definiteness. The boundary between matter and energy has become blurred. Matter has been conceived hitherto as a kind of substance, a kind of thing. Energy, on the other hand, has been conceived not as a substance but as a certain state which can be attributed to a substance. But recent physics blurs the boundary between energy and matter. According to current theories, energy is something that possesses mass and thus an attribute hitherto regarded as an attribute of matter. The capacity to perform a certain amount of work was the state of bodies which was called energy. Recent physics asserts that a body may transform its mass into work and consequently that the mass of a body is also a capacity for doing work and is therefore energy. Consequently matter and energy are, as it were, different forms of one and the same thing: matter may be transformed into energy and *vice versa*. Matter loses its character of substance, that is of a thing.

And furthermore, they say, if we want to penetrate what body essentially is we try to find out what its ultimate components are. Now electrons, nuclei and similar entities, which are thought to be the ultimate components of the bodies given to us in experience, become, in the theories of contemporary physics, something quite dissimilar to what we considered bodies to be. We are no longer allowed to imagine electrons, etc. as little corpuscles, as miniature versions of something that can be seen or touched. Physicists talk as a matter of fact about the spatial dimensions of electrons, protons, neutrons, etc. but these expressions have only a figurative sense. Physicists occasionally say that they wish to give an account of certain experiments with electrons, protons, neutrons, etc. conceived as 'corpuscles', that is as tiny lumps, but when they are concerned with the explanation of experiments of another kind physicists do not consider electrons, etc. to be tiny lumps but talk about them as if they were waves or sets of waves. These waves, however, have no substantial basis, they are not waves of some kind of 'ether' or of anything that can be treated as a thing. Every elongation of such waves in a certain place is only the measure of probability that in this place at a given time there will occur such and such phenomena as, for example, phosphorescence of a screen, the darkening of a photographic plate or similar things. In this way electrons and their microcosmic partners are entirely resolved into abstractions. We reach the summit of abstraction when we hear the physicists' answer to the question what really are these electrons and their companions, which physicists talk about as particles in relation to some experiments and as waves in relation to others. The answer is that physicists know only that in relation to some experiments electrons behave as particles, and thus as tiny lumps, and in relation to other experiments they behave as waves: what they are 'in themselves', however, that is independently of all experiments and observations, this physicists do not know and furthermore they consider the question to be barren, one whose mere formulation excludes the possibility of answering it. To ask what an electron is when we do not observe it, is, according to physicists, as unreasonable as to ask what something is that we do not investigate at all.

Now the defenders of the soul consider these arguments of physicists as profit to their account. Recent physical theories entitle them, they think, to the assertion that matter has been dematerialised, that it has been dissolved into abstractions. Contemporary physics, in their opinion, has shown that the gross matter, known to us as bodies under the jurisdiction of our senses, is only an illusion. Physics has shown that this gross matter is only a form in which complexes of microscopic entities appear, electrons and positrons, nucleons, mesons and neutrinos; these, however, are not real things at all, but abstract entities and as such do not belong to the real world. Of real entities there remain only souls because they alone are irreducible components of the world given to us in experience, that is of nature.

It should be pointed out that the defenders of the soul who choose such a defence leave the dualistic position and adopt a monistic standpoint and acknowledge only spiritual substances. Dualism, as we have seen, regards both bodies and souls as real and substantial components of nature. First of all, we should notice, however, that the arguments sketched above, which lead to the conclusion eliminating bodies from the world of real entities, cannot withstand a critical examination. From the fact that contemporary physics gives up visual models of the elementary particles of bodies and characterises them only abstractly it does not in the least follow that these components are not something real, that is existing in a certain place at a certain time. It follows even less that 'gross matter', that is bodies accessible to our perception, are only an illusion. No physicist can deny the real existence of the bodies given to us in experience; the whole of physical knowledge is based on observations and experiments concerned with these bodies. The results of the investigations of physicists can at most lead us to make certain corrections in our concept of matter, which was formed on the basis of common experience that was neither sufficiently painstaking nor thorough. Materialism, however, is not at all bound to this original concept of matter. This was emphasised at the beginning of the twentieth century by one of the representatives of dialectical materialism, V. I. Lenin, who asserted that it is just the business of the painstaking investigations that physics undertakes to answer the question what in actual fact the world of bodies that is given to us in sensory experience is. Materialism, according to Lenin, asserts only that this world really exists and is not merely a product of our minds or a complex of impressions. In this formulation of its thesis materialism is mainly directed against idealism, which denies an existence independent of our minds to the world of bodies, and not against dualism, which in fact recognises the existence of bodies and demands only the same recognition for souls as substances different from bodies.

*A general characterisation of materialism.* Materialism is, first of all, anti-irrationalistic in its orientation. This means that it will not acknowledge assertions which have not been justified in a way that would be considered sufficient in the special sciences. From this comes its negative attitude towards religion based on revelation, towards traditionally sanctified superstitions that are not supported by any genuine arguments, towards all convictions that arise from our desires, rather than from sober investigations and arguments. Secondly, the materialist standpoint is distinctly realistic; it considers the world given to us in experience to be true reality and not merely a phenomenal phantasm which conceals other things that are in themselves inaccessible to rational cognition. From both these assumptions the materialist conviction follows that the ultimate view of the world must be sought in the results of painstaking investigations, conducted by the natural sciences, benefiting from the powerful arsenal of mathematics. This means that the nature with which the natural sciences acquaint us is for materialists not only true reality but the only reality. Apart from nature there is no world of things in themselves such as idealists would persuade us of and there is not beyond nature any supernatural world such as religion wants to tell us about by appealing to revelation as contained in traditional superstitions, which are demanded by our desires and the needs of our hearts, which appeal to our premonitions and feelings, but have no support from sober reason. This is the basic content of the materialist doctrine. In this framework the controversy about the soul, which occupies such a large place in the history of materialism, is only a fragment which by itself would not be very important. The problem whether that which thinks is a body, that is, whether it has spatial characteristics and inertia or whether it does not, is itself a problem of no great importance and is difficult to solve by means of scientific methods. This controversy has, however, played an important role in the history of materialism because, first, the opponents of materialism made use of idealistic arguments in this dispute and, secondly, the believers in a supernatural world made the soul out to be that component of nature which linked it to the supernatural world, the true homeland of the soul, which abides only temporarily on the earth.

This conception of the soul must be resisted by materialism which does not recognise the supernatural world; the soul, on the other hand, as a component of nature and confined to it, would not be contradictory of the basic tenets of the materialistic doctrine.

*The relation of physical to mental phenomena.* The controversy about the soul, conceived as a substance in which mental phenomena take place, can arise only if we assume that mental phenomena are distinct from physical ones. This difference is recognised not only by the proponents of substantial dualism but also by the dialectical version of materialism. It is denied, however, by mechanical materialism, which emphasises the close relation between physical phenomena on the one hand and the phenomena of consciousness on the other. This relation consists of the fact that each mental phenomenon corresponds in a one-to-one manner to a certain physiological phenomenon; however, this relation is differently interpreted by those who see a difference between mental phenomena and their physiological equivalents. Some, for instance, assume that physiological phenomena are the causes of the corresponding mental phenomena. Some in addition to this accept that sometimes the reverse relation obtains, that mental phenomena can cause physiological ones. The view which accepts mutual determination of mental and physiological phenomena is known as *interactionism*. The view which maintains that only physiological phenomena influence mental ones, and not *vice versa*, and, furthermore, that mental phenomena are not connected among themselves by direct causal relations, is known as *epiphenomenalism*: on this view mental phenomena are only, so to speak, by-products, the faint reflections of physiological phenomena. Some subscribe to the hypothesis of *parallelism,* according to which physiological phenomena do not cause mental ones and nor does the reverse relation obtain, but that series of both these kinds of phenomena occur side by side in a parallel fashion, a given phenomenon in one series corresponding to a given phenomenon in the other, and *vice versa*, although they are not connected by causal relations. There is finally the *double aspect theory* according to which physiological phenomena and the mental phenomena corresponding to them are not really two different kinds of phenomena but are only two different aspects of one and the same phenomenon. The same real process, when contemplated by the individual in whom it takes place by means of introspection, has the character of a mental phenomenon, when inspected, on the other hand, by means of the outer senses (for example, by the physiologist who examines nervous currents in the brain) it has the character of a physiological phenomenon. But neither the one nor the other of these aspects is truer than the other, just as the visual aspect of a marble sphere lying in front of me is not truer than its tactual aspect when I take the sphere in my hand.

*Emotional sources of opposition to materialism.* The controversy about the soul is seldom a dispassionate one. It is not devoid of emotional resonance. It seems to us that the recognition of ourselves and our fellow men as merely bodies lowers our dignity, reduces us to the rank of pawns dependent merely on the play of natural forces and that it deprives us of the autonomy, independence and freedom to which we aspire. It seems that to consider us, people, as among the bodies of nature dispels as an illusion everything that we regard as sublime and noble about ourselves, cancels our higher feelings and aspirations, our ideals. It deprives us finally of the faith that we shall not perish after death, the faith that the people we love who are gone still exist, although not among embodied entities, that our separation from them is only a temporary one.

This autonomy of ours, if it is thought to consist in self-mastery, in our control of physical impulses, in our ability to subordinate lower aims to higher ones, is not questioned by materialism at all; if it is thought to consist in the total independence of our mind from natural forces, it is, of course, a fiction. Nor does materialism cancel what is noble and sublime in us. It does not transform us into dead bodies, but recognises us as bodies animated by mental life; it does not deny the existence of our mental life, although (as regards mechanical materialism) it takes a different view about the essence of this life. It does deprive us, however, of faith in life after death. It is in this that lies the tragical quality of the doctrine which makes it unacceptable to many. Furthermore, materialism on a cosmic scale is incompatible with all religions. Emotional factors which support religion are thus opposed to materialism which limits existence to the totality of natural objects.

*Spiritualism.* As we have already mentioned, both dualism and materialism are forms of realism. The idealist position (particularly subjective idealism) is connected with *spiritualism*. The spiritualistic thesis asserts that in the real world only spiritual substances exist. This thesis is held, first of all, by the adherents of subjective idealism and especially those of immanent idealism. If, according to this form of idealism, bodies are only complexes of impressions, and thus are certain states of the subject of consciousness, then they cannot pretend to be self-subsistent beings, that is substances. Self-subsistent being is possessed only by conscious subjects, that is by souls. Spiritualism of this kind can be called idealistic spiritualism.

However, spiritualism does not necessarily have to be bound up with subjective idealism. We can find a realistic version of spiritualism in the history of philosophy. This kind of spiritualism assumes that spiritual substances alone really exist and that there are no other substances. However, bodies exist as well, but bodies are only manifestations of spiritual substance. This view is expressed by Leibniz in his monadology. According to this view, the ultimate bricks in the construction of the world are what he calls monads, that is souls. Among them are some which possess conscious life, and these alone are what are ordinarily called souls, but there are others as well, which have only a subconscious mental life and these, and complexes of them, are what are ordinarily called bodies.

Spiritualism is attacked by both materialism and dualism, but this attack is mainly directed against the idealistic version of spiritualism and it takes the form of a battle between realism and subjective idealism.

*Monism proper: the identity theory.* Both spiritualism and materialism can be included among *monistic trends,* that is trends which recognise only one kind of substance, in contra-distinction to dualism, which recognises two kinds. Among monistic trends are also to be found what is called *monism proper,* known also as *the theory of identity of soul and body.* The inventor of this metaphysical position was the Jewish philosopher Baruch Spinoza, who lived in Holland in the seventeenth century. The thesis of monism proper asserts that *only one kind of substance exists and it possesses both spiritual and bodily attributes.* Bodiliness and spirituality are only two different aspects through which one and the same substance manifests itself. Neither of the two aspects is more real than the other.

*Immanent monism.* All these trends, which seek to find substance in souls or in bodies or both in souls and bodies, and, finally, in something which is just as much soul as body, are opposed by the trend that holds that neither souls nor bodies are the ultimate bricks out of which nature is constructed. The originator of this view was David Hume. According to him, both bodies and souls are merely complexes of elements given to us in direct experience such as colours, scents, sounds, tastes, pains, feelings of pleasure, etc. Hume related his views to those of Berkeley, who maintained that bodies are merely complexes of impressions. Souls, however, Berkeley considered to be things which are aware of impressions and other mental states but are things distinct from these states. The soul is the subject of mental phenomena. Now Hume emphasised that Berkeley was not wholly consistent. Considering what the bodies we perceive are, Berkeley arrived at the view that our bodies are nothing but complexes of colours, shapes, scents, tastes, etc. and thus complexes of impressions and that they can be nothing else if they are to be perceptible. Hume observes that if Berkeley were to apply a similar course of reasoning to the soul he would have come to a similar conclusion, namely that the soul is only a bundle of mental experiences, is a stream of consciousness. Nothing beyond our own mental states is given to us in experience. In particular, no mysterious subject of these phenomena is given to us in addition to mental phenomena, that is no soul is given to us in experience. On this account Hume maintains that neither souls nor bodies exist as substances. *Neither souls nor bodies are substances*; they are only complexes of certain elements which are either actual contents of consciousness, or can by their nature become such contents. The contents of consciousness are called immanent entities. For this reason the view just sketched can be called *immanent monism*.

Immanent monism can assume two forms: spiritualistic or neutral. It takes on a spiritualistic form when it asserts that these elements, these colours, sounds, tastes, etc. can exist only as contents of consciousness, when it thus takes them to be something mental. It takes a neutral form when these elements are considered to be something that does not have to be the content of consciousness but can exist unrelated to anyone's consciousness (cf. pp. 77f).

### Determinism and indeterminism

*The controversy about the causal constitution of nature.* The question whether the course of events occurring in nature is subordinated to laws by which the entire present and future are determined with inevitable necessity by the past or whether, on the contrary, there are events which are not caused by any earlier event has been the theme of persistent philosophical controversies. This problem could be more concisely expressed as: does every event occur as the inevitable consequence of a certain cause or are there events which are the effects of no cause? The assertion claiming that every event is the effect of some cause is known as *the principle of causality*. The controversy under discussion, then, is concerned with the universal validity of the principle of causality. The ascription of universal validity to the principle of causality, and therefore the assertion claiming that every event is the effect of a cause, is called *determinism*; the denial of universal validity to the principle of causality, and thus the assertion that not everything in the world is the effect of a cause, is called *indeterminism*.

*Analysis and criticism of the concept of cause.* The concept of the causal relation is one of the very general concepts which ontology has attempted to make more precise. The point is that this concept is, if closely examined, by no means clear. By the cause of a given phenomenon is understood the factor which, through its activity, brings about this phenomenon, which is as it were the agent producing it. We understand very well what it means to say that we bring something about ourselves by our activity; we understand what it means to say that we ourselves produce something. But these concepts of activity and production which we apply to ourselves undoubtedly contain certain psychological elements; it is not only outer experience, not only observation of the movements of my body, that informs me that at a given moment I am acting and through this bringing about such and such a phenomenon, but also introspection. In order to assert that it is I who am acting, I must feel a muscular effort and be aware that this effort is directed by my will. Of course, we do not speak about the activity of non-living objects in the same sense as that in which we talk about our own activity. No-one, surely, would wish to assert that a billiard ball, which on impact initiates the movement of another, acts in the sense of the word in which we use it when we talk about our own activity; no-one would maintain that it exerts an effort consciously and wants to move the other ball. But in what sense then do we use the word 'acts' when talking about non-living bodies as active causes?

Perhaps in order to explain the concept of 'action' we should resort to the concept of 'force' and accept the following definition: '*X* acts on *Y*' means the same as '*X* exerts force on *Y*'. But is the concept of 'force' sufficiently clear itself? Force has usually been defined as that which acts or as that which is the cause of change. If we define 'force' in this way, however, we should commit a vicious circle in the definition of the concept of 'action' or the concept of 'cause' which we previously explained in terms of the concept of force. We could, bearing in mind the physical concept of 'force', attempt the following definition: a force acts on a body if and only if this body changes its speed or undergoes deformation. This definition of force would account only for mechanical phenomena and would not be useful for defining either the concept of 'action' or the concept of 'cause' which we apply not only to mechanical phenomena but to other physical phenomena and even to mental ones.

Therefore the attempt to explain the concept of 'cause' through the concept of 'action' or through the concept of 'force' turns out to be unsatisfactory. Because of this, attempts have been made to explain cause without using the concepts of action or force. The cause of a given phenomenon has been described as that after which a given phenomenon must necessarily follow. But here again the question arises what is meant by 'must necessarily'? How shall we recognise whether phenomenon $A$ simply follows phenomenon $B$ or whether phenomenon $A$ had necessarily to follow phenomenon $B$? And here critical analysis of the concept of necessity has shown that this concept is by no means clear. Let us consider why it is that we say that a stone released from the hand must fall down and a bullet fired from a gun does not have to hit the target. The fact that this stone if released from the hand will fall down we consider to be a necessary phenomenon because we know that this always happens; on the other hand, the fact that the bullet fired from a gun will hit the target we do not consider to be necessary because we know that this does not always happen. Because of these examples the following definition of necessity suggests itself: phenomenon $B$ must happen after the phenomenon $A$ means the same as the occurrence of the phenomenon $B$ after the phenomenon $A$ is a particular case of a general law. Some are indeed satisfied with such a definition of the necessary succession of phenomena after each other which reduces it to their regular sequence. However, this definition of 'necessity' will be of no avail for the definition of the causal relation. If we call phenomenon $A$ the cause of phenomenon $B$ when phenomenon $B$ must necessarily follow after phenomenon $A$, then if we reduce necessary succession to regular succession, we shall have to recognise phenomenon $A$ as the cause of phenomenon $B$ when $B$ always follows after $A$. In that case we shall have to recognise the passage of one train through a station as the cause of the passage of another train if, according to the timetable, the second always comes after the first; but this is not at all what we mean by the causal relation.

Attempts have been made to grasp the essence of the causal relation by defining the necessary succession of phenomena not as any regular succession but as regular succession following from fundamental laws of nature, and not from conventions (such as a timetable). Attempts to determine more precisely what these fundamental laws of nature are run into insurmountable difficulties.

*The problem of prediction.* As a result of these considerations and difficulties, a tendency has emerged to eliminate the concept of cause from the apparatus of scientific concepts. For this reason the original formulation of the problem of determinism has been given up and new formulations have been attempted. The problem of determinism in the realm of the natural sciences has been formulated recently without using the word 'cause', without applying such terms as 'necessity', 'inevitable effect', etc. The current formulation of the problem of determinism in the natural sciences takes approximately the following form: 'Can the course of events occurring in nature be expressed in laws which enable us to predict future events on the basis of the observable qualities of the events that have hitherto taken place?' The problem of determinism thus takes the form of 'predictionism' (predictability). It is now no longer concerned with the determination of the future by the past but rather with whether we can predict the future on the basis of the past.

In the period when mechanism dominated the natural sciences, that is when the view prevailed that all phenomena of corporeal nature could be explained by the laws of mechanics, the natural sciences upheld the deterministic position. The most emphatic expression of this determinism was given by Laplace, a French scientist of the second part of the eighteenth century, who asserted that an intellect of unlimited capacities for the solution of theoretical problems (the case in point was the solution of differential equations of the second order), who knew the laws of nature (Laplace had in mind the laws of Newtonian mechanics) and who knew at a given moment the positions and velocities of all the material points making up the world, could, from these data and in accordance with these laws, deduce what will be or have been their positions and velocities at every future and past moment. Knowledge of the state of nature at a given time would thus enable one who knows the laws of nature (the laws of Newtonian mechanics) to deduce the whole of the future and the past. Laplace assumed at the same time that what we need to know of the present in order to deduce the past and the future from it (the position and velocity of all material points) is accessible in principle to cognition. The subsequent development of physics has undermined the determinism that Laplace professed. Current quantum theory shows that the laws of physics do not permit us from observed data concerning the ultimate components of matter (electrons, protons, etc.) to deduce their future states. The point is that we are unable to observe all the data we should have to know in order to predict the destiny of particular electrons from them in accordance with the laws of physics. Physics informs us that it is sufficient for calculating the future to know the position and velocity of electrons at a given moment but that it is not sufficient for this prediction to know only one of these parameters, we have to know both. However, because of the very nature of the phenomena, we cannot measure both the velocity and the position of a given electron with the desired accuracy. We can observe only certain average values of parameters as they relate to very large numbers of electrons and from these averages we can compute, according to the laws of statistics, average values which these parameters will assume in future. Thus the destiny of particular electrons cannot be predicted; what can, however, be predicted is the average destiny of large numbers of electrons.

*Are the laws of nature only statistical laws?* Connected with this is a peculiar view advanced by certain scientists about the essence of the laws previously known as causal laws. These laws were usually concerned with the behaviour of larger bodies made of huge numbers of elementary particles of matter. The behaviour of such a body will depend on the average behaviour of all the particles of which it is made, but the behaviour of a single particle will not have much influence on the behaviour of the whole mass. Now if we are dealing with the mass of events, there must occur in this mass certain statistical regularities, even if particular components of the events occur quite irregularly and capriciously. For this reason the behaviour of larger bodies which are aggregates of huge numbers of elementary particles must, as mass events, be governed by statistical regularities, even if the behaviour of these elementary particles were quite irregular. Hence the suggestion presents itself that the laws governing phenomena in which larger bodies participate can be reduced to statistical laws. Any regularity in the world, previously considered to be a manifestation of a mysterious causality governing the world, would be, according to this view, only a statistical regularity, concealing nothing mysterious within it. This regularity occurs only if we are dealing with huge numbers of elementary particles. But in the world of these particles complete chaos reigns and the absence of any regularity. The view of the essence of the laws of nature sketched above – accepted by everybody with regard to some physical laws (e.g. the laws of thermodynamics) – is questioned as a general view which attempts to reduce all the laws of nature to statistical laws (except for those which simply follow from the content of the concepts used in them and thus are only analytic judgements).

*Freedom of the will*. With the problem of determinism another, by no means emotionally indifferent, one has often been connected, namely the problem of the *freedom of the will*. The freedom of the will, which is the problem at issue, has not always been seen in the same way. Sometimes freedom of man's will has been conceived in terms of his ability to be faithful to what he considers to be most worthy of his efforts and thus his ability to resist any temptation which tends to lead him astray. The freedom of the will so conceived, one of the most remarkable features of human character, should rather be called the strength of the will than its freedom.

But other meanings have also been attached to the term 'freedom of the will'. The most important of them is that connected with the problem of causality which we have just considered. On this interpretation the question whether the human will is free is reduced to the question whether the acts of the human will are unequivocally determined by certain causes or not. The point is whether a man equipped with a certain character, dispositions and predilections, must, as the result of certain motives, make specific decisions or whether a man of a given character can, as a result of given motives, decide one way or the other. Thus the problem of the freedom of the will is concerned with the question whether the human will is subordinated to the general principle of causality or whether it escapes from its constraints, whether the acts of the human will are merely intermediate links in causal chains, having both causes and effects, or whether they are only the beginnings of causal chains and although they have effects, have no causes. The recognition of the human will as free in the above sense seems to be required by human dignity which seems to be diminished by the thought that man is merely an element of nature doomed to the favours and disfavours of forces prevailing in it which he cannot resist. Situations in which a strong man resists temptations, combats base motives, seem to demonstrate that man is capable of being his own master and of opposing the forces of nature. It would seem, finally, that the freedom of the will is a condition without which it is impossible to hold man morally responsible for his deeds. It has been thought that if the human will is not free, that if men were equipped by nature with an innate character and dispositions, he would not be able, given certain motives, to make a choice, but would have to behave in a certain way, that and no other, and he would not then be an agent responsible for his deeds but only an automaton carrying out what follows necessarily from his nature. The responsibility for a man's deeds would not then fall on him but on whatever had given him this and no other nature.

These were, it seems, the main motives prompting philosophers to make the human will an exception to the principle of universal causality. These matters have often been discussed in philosophy. The freedom of the will has had its supporters but also its opponents, who argued that the fact of what is called mastery over oneself can be perfectly well reconciled with the assumption that all man's decisions are unequivocally determined by certain conditions and that moral responsibility can be conceived in such a way as not to require the freedom of the will.

*The problem of the existence of the future.* We have so far discussed the problem of determinism as the problem concerned with the causal determination of the future by the past, or of the predictability of the future on the basis of the past. In the history of philosophy this problem has also had a different interpretation connected with the essence of time. It is not easy to give an account of the content of this problem in simple words. Perhaps it could be best presented by resorting to a metaphor. Greek mythology tells of Kronos, chief of the Titans, who seized power over the world from his father Uranus and, wanting to escape the fate he had arranged for his father, killed and ate his children after they were born. Now Kronos is supposed to be the embodiment of time (*chronos* means 'time' in Greek), his relationship to his own children is supposed to express figuratively the essence of time, at once the creator and destroyer of his own creations. Every happy or unhappy event is called into life and being by time, but immediately it has started to exist time pushes it into the past and it ceases to exist.

But is it the case that what has become past has ceased to exist? Perhaps it still endures and exists and has only slipped away from our eyes as roadside trees disappear from our eyes as we travel along a road at a good speed. Perhaps, even, future events are already waiting for us as a distant landscape waits for a traveller, still invisible, hidden by the mists of distance. Perhaps it is we who are unable to look along this road on which the course of our life unrolls because our sight is limited by a curtain which lets us see the road only perpendicularly and allows us to see only what we are passing. Perhaps some other entity whose sight is not limited by this kind of curtain can see what we have just passed and also what awaits us on our way, in addition to what we are just passing. Perhaps, then, the privileged position which we ascribe to the present, the distinction that we draw between what is now and what was or will be, is the result of people's peculiar way of looking at the world. In the real world there may be no difference between the mode of existence of what is now, what was before and what will be in the future. Perhaps past, present and future are ready from the beginning of the world and the difference which we envisage in their existence is merely a subjective difference, connected with the organisation of our minds.

This is a second problem which is called the problem of determinism. We have attempted to convey it to the reader, using expressions and terms for which we should not like to be held responsible. The question here is whether the future is already arranged now, whether of two contradictory statements of which one asserts that a certain fact will occur in the future and the second denies it, one is already true and the other false or perhaps neither of them is now either true or false and they will only become one or the other when the proper moment arrives. Those who believe that the whole is and always has been arranged but was merely absent subscribe to determinism of a certain kind; those who assume that the future is not yet arranged, that only time creates it, subscribe to indeterminism. The problem just discussed was raised in recent times by the French philosopher H. Bergson, who adhered to indeterminism so conceived, seeing time as the creator of the real world (*temps créateur*), and, in the history of the world, creative evolution (*évolution créatrice*).

## Mechanism and finalism

*The controversy about the purposive arrangement of the world.* Is the world *purposively* arranged or does it just roll blindly ahead? This is a general formulation of the problem to which mechanism replies negatively and finalism affirmatively. The position called *finalism* or *teleology* assumes that the world is arranged purposively, mechanism on the other hand denies it. The expressions 'teleology' and 'finalism' are derived from the Greek word *telos* and the Latin word *finis* which correspond to the English word 'purpose'. Mechanism represents the tendency opposed to teleology because its adherents think that the course of all phenomena in the world occurs as if in a mechanism and is not directed by purpose in the way that human conduct is.

*Anthropomorphic purposiveness.* The finalistic view may assume an anthropomorphic form or some other. Anthropomorphic finalism, maintaining that the world is purposively arranged, takes this to mean that the world is the purposeful deed of an entity capable of thought, desire and the realisation of its will, and that it is constructed by this entity for a certain purpose. The adherents of this view seem to be convinced that in nature there are many features that cannot be explained except by accepting the hypothesis that they were created by an intelligent and omnipotent being in order to fulfil certain aspirations which are consciously felt by this entity.

Anthropomorphic finalism, taking the whole world to be the product of an entity which aims at a certain purpose (or purposes), is connected with the idea that there is an individual God, the creator and ruler of the world.

As can be seen, anthropomorphic finalism belongs to the metaphysical trends bound up with religion rather than results from the investigation of nature. From these investigations a trend in opposition to anthropomorphic finalism more often arises, that is philosophical mechanism which maintains that to explain the phenomena of nature we do not need a hypothesis that the world is the product of a Creator seeking to fulfil his aspirations.

Finalism asserts that the number of facts which cannot be understood except as the manifestations of the purposeful activity of a Creator is vast. They can be found in inorganic as well as in organic nature. In nature, the finalists argue, we do not find conditions making organic life possible everywhere but find them exclusively on the earth. We also come across certain deviations from the regularities that prevail in nature without which life, or some of its forms at least, would be impossible. Thus, for example, all liquids, with the exception of water, become denser when cooled, but water alone becomes densest at the temperature of 4 degrees centigrade and becomes less dense both when it is heated and when it is cooled. To this extraordinary characteristic of water we owe the fact that in freezing weather rivers and lakes do not freeze throughout but are covered with a layer of ice beneath which water temperature of +4 degrees centigrade, is maintained. In this water fish and other organisms can survive which would otherwise die if the whole of the water was transformed into ice. This is an example, one of many, of exceptions from the regularities of nature without which life would be impossible. Is not this exceptional equipment of the earth with conditions which are favourable to the life of organisms, and, furthermore, are not these exceptions to natural regularities without which life could not exist, sufficient evidence that the Creator of the world purposefully arranged the world in such a way and deliberately established certain deviations from natural regularities so that life could emerge and survive on the earth?

This is one of the lines of thought developed by finalists. Let us consider whether it can be logically defended. If I come across a hut made of wood in the mountains which can give shelter from rain and wind, I conclude that someone built this hut in order to serve this purpose for people. It strikes us at first glance that, in the same way that we conclude from the usefulness of the hut that someone has constructed it for this purpose, we can conclude from circumstances advantageous to living entities in nature that it follows that a Creator purposively established them for the benefit of these organic entities. However, the similarity of these two lines of reasoning is merely apparent. If I did not know that people build such huts in the mountains for this purpose before I came across such a hut, I should not have concluded that this hut was built on purpose by someone. My reasoning in the case of the hut belongs to the kind that logic describes as reasoning by analogy. The mere fact of coming across an exceptional arrangement of things which is advantageous does not yet provide a basis for inferring that this arrangement has been purposively created by someone to yield this advantage. If I came across a pyramid of huge rocks in the mountains under which there was a niche, which could, like the hut, serve as a shelter, I should not have concluded from this exceptional and advantageous arrangement of things that someone had purposively arranged these huge rocks so that they would protect me in case of rain. Now the argument of the finalists is similar to this latter, illegitimate, reasoning and not to the former which concerned the hut. Inferring from the advantageous way things are arranged on the earth for living organisms that a Creator arranged things for living organisms in this way we are not reasoning by analogy. The point is we do not know any case in which a similar set of relations as the one the finalists want to regard as the purposive deed of a Creator was deliberately created by someone for the benefit of someone else. The reasoning of finalists assumes an implicit premise that whenever we come across a set of conditions differing from the normal which is advantageous for someone or something living, this set is the purposive product of a benevolent entity. This premise is, of course, false, because by applying it from the fact that the dealer has dealt someone exceptionally good cards we could draw the conclusion that he did it deliberately, being well-disposed toward the fortunate player or that some benevolent spirits well-disposed towards this player have influenced the dealing of the cards. By using this premise we could also deduce that because of the damp in the cellar of a house which makes possible the existence of mould in this cellar the builder of the house deliberately tried to create this dampness so that the mould could flourish. Of course, these conclusions are absurd and so is the premise on which they are based.

It is quite clear that whenever we come across organic life some conditions must have been satisfied to make it possible. Thus it is legitimate to say that life exists because of these conditions. However, before we establish independently that these conditions have been deliberately arranged by someone benevolently disposed to these living organisms, we have no right to say that in this case these conditions were created by someone in order to make organic life possible.

As evidence of the purposeful arrangement of the world finalists cite, first of all, the constitution of organic entities and their extraordinary adaptability to the conditions of life. Using countless examples they show how extraordinarily complex, subtle and harmonious an apparatus every organism is. They show furthermore how extraordinarily 'wise' this apparatus is, that is they show that the organism, because of its structure, is perfectly adapted to changing conditions of life and for this reason can survive and transmit this form of life to its descendants until the external circumstances become catastrophic for it. Now the adherents of finalism think that apparatuses that are so ingenious and so perfectly adapted to external conditions could not have arisen as the result of 'chance', but must have been the deed of a creator who deliberately gave them this 'wise' structure, so that they could live and continue their species.

This view is not shared by philosophical mechanism whose adherents think that the emergence of even the most ingenious organisms, equipped with the constitutions which enable them to survive and transmit life to their species, can be explained without resorting to the hypothesis of the purposive activity of a Creator. The theory which attempts to explain the origin of organisms that are so wonderfully adapted to the conditions of life without appealing to supernatural factors is the theory of the struggle for survival created by Charles Darwin. According to this theory (corrected by later opinions) as a result of the influence of certain external circumstances it sometimes happens that certain changes occur in the reproductive cells of certain organisms as the result of which the immediate progeny of these organisms receive a new characteristic differentiating them from their parents and this characteristic is transmitted to subsequent generations. The new characteristic may be advantageous to the progeny in the struggle for existence, but it may also be harmful or indifferent, in other words, the progeny may become better adapted to life but may also be worse or equally adapted. Now it is quite clear that, if among later generations there are variations better adapted to life, these rather than others will survive and reproduce themselves. In the struggle for existence those variations win which are better adapted. In this way, in the course of time, ancestors less adapted to life are replaced by those of their descendants who are able to cope with the conditions of life better than they, rather than by those who are less well adapted. Thus organisms emerge that are more and more highly organised, equipped with the ever more complex apparatus which enables them to cope with an ever more varied range of conditions.

Without denying that the development of organisms could have happened in the way suggested by the theory of the struggle for existence, the adherents of finalism argue that it is infinitely improbable that we could explain all the details of an apparatus of higher organisms that is so extraordinarily complex and so accurately adjusted to the conditions of life in this way. How many of these chance variations, they ask, would have had to happen so that among countless harmful and indifferent variations could have occurred all these advantageous ones which were required for the emergence of the wonderful apparatuses we find in the organic world and which infinitely exceed any product of human invention. Such an accumulation of chances seems infinitely improbable. In reply to this objection we may observe that nature has at its disposal almost infinite time for the production of the organisms now living. The birth of a calf with two heads is a rare phenomenon and because of this it is improbable that it will occur once again in a given region in a given year. It is more probable, however, that it will recur within two years, still more probable that this event will happen again within a hundred years and still more probable that it will occur during a thousand years. If we regard all these variations that are required, according to the theory of the struggle for existence, for the explanation of the emergence of the organisms living today as infinitely improbable we perhaps judge this probability too little because of a perspectival shortening of the time in which all these variations occur.

*Biological mechanism and vitalism.* Philosophical mechanism, which simply asserts that for the explanation of the phenomena of nature we do not have to resort to the hypothesis of the purposive arrangement of the world by a deliberately acting Creator, should not be confused with biological mechanism. The main thesis of biological mechanism is the view that, for the explanation of the phenomena of organic nature, those laws are sufficient which are necessary and sufficient for the explanation of inorganic nature and that therefore all biological laws can be inferred from the laws of physics and chemistry. The trend opposite to biological mechanism is vitalism, which maintains that the laws governing inorganic nature are not sufficient for giving an account of the facts of the organic world and that therefore physico-chemical laws are not sufficient for the explanation of all biological phenomena.

Vitalism in its original form, that is palaeovitalism, assumed that the course of organic processes was directed by so-called vital powers or by mysterious entities called archeuses which steer the physical energy provided for the organism from outside in such a way that the organism can survive and develop. However, it was only in the most primitive form of this palaeovitalism that it was held that this steerer of the organism is an entity which consciously aims at some purpose. This position inclined towards that of anthropomorphic finalism but only as regards organisms in their organic form and not as regards the world as a whole. Although the contemporary form of vitalism appeals to the participation of such factors as dominants, entelechies, psychoids, etc. which guide the course of phenomena in the organic world in accordance with laws quite different from those governing inorganic nature, the adherents of this neovitalism clearly disavow the treatment of these entelechies, psychoids, etc. as entities consciously aiming at certain purposes. Vitalism, and particularly contemporary vitalism, is far removed from anthropomorphic finalism.

The position closest to anthropomorphic finalism is psychovitalism, which maintains that the whole of living nature, each of its cells, every organism, is endowed with a soul which aims towards development, the preservation of the organism, etc. but it aims towards these ends in an unconscious way. We find echoes in psychovitalism of Leibniz's teaching about monads and of Fechner's philosophy which regards the entire universe and its components as equipped with souls. Both Leibniz and Fechner were adherents of the finalistic position.

*A non-anthropomorphic concept of purposive constitution.* Not all the philosophical trends that are called finalistic have taken the form of anthropomorphic finalism. Aristotle's finalism, for instance, was not anthropomorphic. That philosopher, when he talked about the 'principles of causes of being', distinguished four kinds and among them efficient and final causes. By efficient cause, he understood more or less what is commonly meant by cause. The final cause was meant to be the 'form' actualising itself in the developing object (cf. p. 103). When we consider the developing organism of an insect which, after it is hatched from an egg, takes the form of a larva, then of a chrysalis and finally takes its perfect shape, then its 'form' is the final perfect shape which an insect normally assumes at the final stage of its development. Now, according to Aristotle, it is the form, the perfect shape, which is realised, in favourable circumstances, at the end of the developmental process, which influences the course of this process and which leads and directs it. This form, of course, belongs to the world of abstractions (Platonic ideas) and is not an event or a thing in the real world. Aristotle does not think, however, that the embodiment of this form in a developing organism is purposive in an anthropomorphic sense, that is in the sense of someone's consciously desiring to create this embodiment and the whole developmental process so as to make possible the embodiment of this form in this organism. This form or its embodiment is not, therefore, the purpose of the development in a literal sense, but in a figurative sense which is not clearly elucidated by Aristotle. The analogy between the figurative and literal meanings of 'purpose' consists in the fact that in much the same way as a purpose in the literal sense comes at the end of a process of action as its consummation, this embodiment of a form, its perfect shape, in an organism comes (in normal circumcumstances) at the end of the developmental process as its consummation. According to Aristotle this last phase of the process which appears normally at the end of its development 'acts' as if it were attracting the whole organism to itself. Because of its 'action' Aristotle calls it a cause and because it does not precede the process but consists (normally) of its final phase, he calls it the final cause (in contrast to the earlier efficient cause).

Now Aristotle thought that everywhere, whenever something happens, besides efficient causes, which are not sufficient for the explanation of phenomena, there are also final causes, that is purposes (in a figurative sense). The entire course of events in the world, that is the world as a whole, conceived as a gigantic and extraordinarily complex process developing in time, also possesses its final cause. The final cause of the world is, as with organisms, its form. The form of the world, to which realisation the world tends in its development, is called by Aristotle God. God moves the world, as Aristotle says, not as an 'impeller' (*hos kinumenos*) but as the object of love (*hos eromenos*), as the purpose of striving.

*Neovitalists.* Figurative thinking about purposiveness like Aristotle's is to be found in some contemporary vitalists. They assert that processes occurring in organisms are purposive in the sense that we cannot predict their course when we know only earlier conditions and that we must know the final phase which the individuals of the species to which a given organism belongs assume in their development in normal conditions. It is only this final phase of the development of the organisms of a given species (a concept close to the concept of form in Aristotle), together with preceding conditions and those concurrent with particular phases of development, that 'determine' its real course.

Now suppose an experimental scientist cuts off the tails and right back legs of two lizards. After a time regenerative tissues appear on the wounded spots. In one lizard a tail develops from the tissues growing at the place of the tail, a leg from the tissues growing at the place of the leg. However, the second lizard undergoes another experiment: the tissue from which the tail was to grow is transplanted to the place where the leg was, and the tissue from which the leg was to grow is transplanted to the place where the tail was. It might be expected that after the second experiment from this second lizard a monster would grow with a leg in place of the tail and a tail in place of the leg, but even the second lizard assumes its normal shape after a time. The course of this experiment shows, according to vitalists, that what develops from the regenerative tissue is not decided by its chemical and cytological structure. The point is that from the same tissue from which the first lizard grew a tail, the second lizard grew a leg, and *vice versa*. It is evident that the same part of the organism develops differently in different conditions. We cannot predict its development from its composition or its structure. We can say only this: in different conditions it will develop differently but always in such a way that in the final phase there will emerge an animal of the normal shape. We have to refer to this normal shape, attainable only at the end of the developmental process, if we want to give laws describing the way the process occurs. Without knowledge of the final phase of development we cannot predict the course of development. In this sense we can say that the normal shape which an organism assumes at the end of its development acts retrogressively in time and guides the course of earlier developmental phases.

The course of the developmental process in an organism seen in this light is like a course of human action directed by a previously established purpose. When a boat is sailing, steered by a sailor towards a certain destination, it reacts to various currents and winds, it moves its rudder and sails in this and that way, but always so that the intended destination is reached as a result. The destination lying in the future to which the sailor consciously strives thus influences his present behaviour, future events influence earlier ones. No-one, unless he knows the destination, will be able to predict the behaviour of the sailor in steering the boat. Similarly, according to vitalists, the behaviour of a developing organism cannot be predicted if we do not know its normal state at the end of its development. This similarity between an organic developmental process and the purposive activity of man, the similarity, consisting of the fact that, just as we cannot predict the behaviour of a man who acts with a certain purpose unless we know what the purpose he is pursuing is, so we cannot predict the course of an organic development without knowledge of what is normally the final shape of the animal, induces some vitalists to call organic processes purposive processes. Calling these processes purposive they do not take this purposiveness in its literal, anthropomorphic sense but rather give the term a figurative meaning, having only some analogies with anthropomorphic purposiveness.

*Holism.* The arguments above draw our attention to yet another peculiar feature appearing in the thought of contemporary students of nature, particularly biologists and psychologists, a feature that is highly significant for ideas about the structure of nature and not devoid of wider significance. The disciplines that deal with non-living nature have accustomed us to the explanation of the behaviour of complex objects by the behaviour of their components. We are accustomed to treat the laws governing the course of complex wholes as following from the laws governing the elements of these wholes. Now contemporary biologists, bearing in mind cases like the one just discussed and many others, come to the conclusion that, as regards living nature, knowledge of the laws governing the elements is not sufficient for inferring the laws governing the wholes that are made up of them; for the understanding of the behaviour of complex wholes we must resort to specific laws that are irreducible to the laws concerning their elements. Furthermore, they think that knowledge of wholes and of the laws that govern them is indispensable for giving an account of the behaviour of the elements. This view, which has many adherents among biologists and psychologists, is called *holism* (from the Greek *holos* = whole). This doctrine, which regards as wholes not only particular animal and vegetable organisms, but also communities and groups made of individual organisms, and asserts that the behaviour of such groups takes place according to laws that are irreducible to laws governing the behaviour of individual organisms, sees in these groups something more than merely a 'sum' of organisms; it sees in them individuals of a higher order, as it were, possessing their own specific life and specific laws. This doctrine could not have failed to have an influence on opinions about the relation between the human individual and society, providing a support in a sense for anti-individualistic tendencies, according a certain primacy to social organisms such as nations and states over human individuals.

The scope of our treatment does not permit us to go beyond this rather sketchy presentation of the views just referred to or to subject them to the critical analysis which they deserve.

*Utilitarian purposiveness.* In addition to the concepts of purposiveness already discussed there is still another in colloquial language. We talk, for instance, about the purposive constitution of living organisms, about their purposive behaviour, etc. If I say, for example, that an animal organism is purposively constituted I do not mean to assert by this that someone has made it so in order to realise a purpose, but simply that it is constituted in a manner that is advantageous for itself and for the species it belongs to. If I say, for example, that the production of colourful flowers by plants that are fertilised by insects is purposive, I do not wish to say that the plants consciously produce flowers in order to achieve a certain pre-established purpose, but I take it to mean that the production of flowers contributes to the survival of the species of this plant. On this interpretation of purposiveness, the purposive is that which contributes to the attainment of a certain value, a certain good. This interpretation of purposiveness we call utilitarian purposiveness.

*Optimism and pessimism.* Now there is another metaphysical problem related to the concept of purposiveness, that of optimism and pessimism. This problem is concerned with the question whether the world is arranged 'purposively', that is in such a way that it contributes to the realisation of this or that good or whether, on the contrary, it obstructs the realisation of this good. The first view is called optimism, the second pessimism. Depending on what value or good we have in mind, we have to deal with different varieties of optimism and pessimism. It may be biological good, that is conditions advantageous for the survival of organisms or biological species. We may ask whether all the details of the constitution of organisms are advantageous for their survival and their normal development in given conditions. The good in question may be happiness. Then the problem of optimism and pessimism is that of whether the arrangement of the world contributes to the achievement of happiness. In this case we are concerned with eudaemonological optimism and pessimism. We may be concerned with moral good and so ask whether the world tends towards the realisation of moral goodness or whether the contrary is the case and moral evil is to prevail in it. Here we are dealing with ethical optimism and pessimism. Finally we can talk about aesthetic optimism and pessimism: the former would hold that beauty prevails in the world, the latter that ugliness prevails.

The problem of optimism and pessimism is usually included in metaphysics but it really lies on the border between metaphysics and this or that axiological discipline (theories of values) and therefore on the border between metaphysics and ethics, metaphysics and aesthetics, etc.

# 10

## Metaphysical problems arising from religion

### The religious concept of deity

Every religion involves beliefs in which the central role is played by the concept of deity. This concept has a different meaning in different religions. In most of them the essential component of the concept of deity is the ascription to it of positive values in the highest degree. Supreme power, wisdom, justice, beauty, etc: these are the characteristics usually connected to the concept of deity. In the polytheistic religions that recognise many gods not all these values are ascribed to one being but are distributed through various deities. In the Greek religion, Zeus was the most powerful, Athena the wisest, Aphrodite the most beautiful, etc. In monotheistic religions all perfections are ascribed to one being. In these religions God is the highest and most perfect being. But not every religion makes this perfection explicit or attempts to single out the attributes which compose it. In some religions, furthermore, it is considered almost blasphemous to try to enumerate God's attributes: blasphemous because the human mind is not capable of ascending to the height at which God dwells. All human attempts to describe the magnificence of God are abortive and every word men use to describe God is inherently inadequate. God is then, according to some religions, too lofty and magnificent to be comprehended and named by man. What then is the content of the concept of God common to all monotheistic religions? What remains it seems is only the emotional content: the highest enthusiasm and respect, humility and submissiveness.

## The immortality of the soul

Connected with faith in God in every religion are certain moral commandments, imposing obligations on people not only in relation to other people but also and above all in relation to God who, according to religious beliefs, rewards the fulfilment of these obligations and punishes failure to fulfil them. Because, as experience teaches, God's justice does not always prevail in the course of an individual's life it is generally assumed in religions that death is not the end of the existence of human individuals but that they still exist after death and that only then in their after-life does the measure of God's justice prevail. This existence after death is conceived differently in different religions. According to some, it consists in the dwelling of souls after death in the place where man achieves the highest happiness because man is face to face with God and reaches the highest moral perfection (saintliness) – or in the place of eternal or temporary and purifying punishment. According to other religions, existence after life consists in another embodiment of the human soul in which it is rewarded or punished. Certain ceremonies are connected with these views, certain rituals, often having the character of a communication with the Highest Being.

## Religious metaphysics

People usually accept religious beliefs under the influence of the environment in which they grow up: their faith usually has a traditional character, is 'the faith of their fathers' in which they are immersed from childhood without any effort on their part to examine these beliefs and opinions. Only a few individuals try to resolve by their own reflection the problems to which ready answers are given by the religious beliefs bequeathed by tradition. Now these independent attempts are usually considered to be a kind of philosophising and they are usually included within the scope of metaphysics. In the practice of religious metaphysics some attempt to apply rational methods, some apply irrational ones. The latter are called mystics.

### The philosophical concept of deity

The two most important metaphysical problems arising from religion are: the problem of God and the problem of the immortality of the soul. In examining the problem of God or gods, metaphysicians sometimes criticise traditional religious opinions which equip the highest and most noble beings with characteristics which are not consistent with this nobility. Thus, for example, Greek philosophers criticised the naive opinions of their religion which personified the forces of nature and elevated these personifications to the pedestal of most noble beings. Xenophanes, a Greek philosopher of the sixth century B.C., ridiculed these anthropomorphisations, maintaining that these were not gods who created people in their own likeness but, on the contrary, that people had created gods in their own likeness and if horses had conceived a religion then horses would be their gods. In place of these naive conceptions of deity the Greek philosophers proposed others. Plato, for instance, calls God the idea of the good, that is of the good in itself. Aristotle identifies as God, that is as the highest being, the form of the world (the formal cause of the world).

Religious metaphysics does not always take a critical standpoint in relation to traditional religion. In the Christian epoch philosophers who examine religious problems generally assume an exegetical attitude towards traditional religion. This means that they do not abandon the concept of deity contained in traditional religion but try to make the content of the concept explicit. So, for example, Christian scholastic philosophy makes the concept of God explicit with the aid of the conceptual apparatus taken from the philosophy of Aristotle, describing God as an entity possessing self-subsistent being and therefore substantial being and, at the same time, as a being distinct from other substances in that, whereas others require a cause in order to exist, it exists by itself, without having any cause of its own existence prior to its existence. God is thus *ens per se et a se existens*. Starting from this conception of God, which the Church accepted as legitimate, seventeenth- and eighteenth-century philosophers elaborated its different variants. In these attempts at giving the traditional concept of God a more explicit content philosophers did not mind if, in making the content more explicit, they departed from the original, highly emotionally charged, concept of deity. In the minds of many religious people this concept is in fact an expression of their longings, their need for a cult, their need to be cared for, an expression of their faith in the meaning of the world and their own life, in the victory of what is good and right – and such a concept could hardly be forced into the dry and cold formulae of rationalistically inclined philosophers. Thus, parallel to these attempts to clarify the content of this main concept of religion, run the arguments of mystics who, abandoning conceptual clarity, develop the emotional aspect of religious experience, using metaphors and pictures, writing religious poems rather than learned treatises.

### Proofs of the existence of God

In addition to attempts to make the traditional concept of

deity explicit, which may be included in the domain of ontology, rationalistically inclined philosophers have made vigorous efforts to prove the existence of God, conceived in one way or another. Among these proofs the most celebrated were: (1) The ontological proof of the existence of God which relies on the fact that in the very concept of the most perfect entity there is contained the attribute of existence, because the most perfect entity if it were non-existent would be less perfect than the most perfect existent entity and therefore would not be the most perfect one. (2) The cosmological proof appeals to the fact that every change in the world must have its cause and that this chain of causes cannot regress *ad infinitum* and that therefore there must be a first cause which has itself no cause and this cause is God, *ens per se et a se existens*. (3) The physico-teleological proof deriving from the fact of the purposive arrangement of the world (purposive in the utilitarian sense) which argues that this arrangement can only be the deed of the wisest and omnipotent entity, that is God. The first of these proofs already met criticism in the middle ages. All these proofs were criticised by Immanuel Kant who tried to show their inadequacy. According to Kant, the existence of God cannot be proved in a theoretical way. It is not an assertion that can be rationally justified but is only a postulate of the practical reason, that is a condition which must be satisfied if morality is to be realised. The mystics, on the other hand, without attempting to give proofs, try to write suggestively so as to implant in others their own religious attitude which arises from deep emotional experience but whose factual content is thoroughly nebulous.

### God and the world

Another theme of great interest to theologically inclined philosophers has been the problem of the relation of God to the world. In traditional religions God, the highest and most sacred entity, is conceived at the same time as the creator of the world. Among philosophers, by and large, he preserves this role. But for some he is only the creator who, having once created the world and having subordinated its course to certain laws, does not interfere in its subsequent destiny and does not disturb the laws of nature established by him before-hand through his own intervention (through miracles). For others he is not only the creator but also Providence, which interferes directly with the fate of the world during the course of its existence. For both these groups, God is some-thing different from the world and is in no sense a component of it. However, the pantheists think otherwise and they identify God with the world or with its substance.

## Atheism

Of course, not all philosophers concerned with religious problems assume a positive attitude towards religious beliefs. There are many who fundamentally oppose religion. Those in particular who deny the existence of God are called atheists. Atheists are, first of all, materialists, with the excep-tion of such materialists as, for example, Stoics who identify God with the world, which they consider to be a material entity, in other words, then, with the exception of materialistic pantheists. For modern materialists all religion is a remnant of the infantile period of humanity, anthropomorphising the forces of nature. They hold that the need to believe in God and his providence exists only in people who have not grown out of this infantile state which prompts us in moments of danger to seek shelter under the fatherly protection of a deity. It is quite clear that, from the standpoint of the defenders of religion, the materialists' attempts to give an explanation of the psychological genesis of religious beliefs have been subjected to a serious criticism which objects to materialists that religion originates in this way only among primitive people while among persons equipped with a richer and deeper inner life religious belief is based on a peculiar kind of profound experience, ignorance of which shows only the poverty of the materialist's spiritual life. Because of the unclarity of the concept of God, that is because of the very different meanings which have been attached to this term in the history of philosophy, the term 'atheism', and equally the names of the trends opposed to atheism, are not unequivocal. This unclarity and mutability of the concept of God has not received enough attention in the history of philosophy.

### The problem of the immortality of the soul among philosophers

The other main theme of speculation in religious metaphysics, as we have already mentioned, is the problem of the immortality of the soul. Religions as a rule affirm a faith in the after-life, but different religions conceive this life in different ways. Independent attempts to deal with this problem are also to be found in metaphysics. As much as the problem of God, this problem is not indifferent from an emotional point of view. The dispute between materialists and the defenders of the soul, in itself cold and dispassionate, takes on flesh and blood because of its connection to the problems of the after-life. As a rule materialists deny this life; the defenders of the soul almost without exception accept it. They attempt at the same time to give arguments allegedly proving the immortality of the soul. Some derive these arguments from reflection on the essence of the soul as something simple and indivisible into parts; others derive them from premises taken from the natural sciences, others again (Kant), rejecting the previous arguments as worthless, consider the immortality of the soul to be simply a postulate which is required by our moral sense, our trust in the realisation of justice and the sanctification of man.

However, the essence of immortality itself has been conceived in various ways. Most philosophers who adhere to the belief in immortality have supposed it to be the persistence of individual souls after death, preserving their consciousness of their identity with this period which we call life. Still others have rejected the individual immortality of the soul, contending that the individualisation of the soul is linked inseparably to the fact of its dwelling within the body. Once liberated from the body the soul loses its individuality and merges itself into the soul of the human species, common to everyone. This, for example, was the opinion of certain Aristotelian commentators who developed his view that the soul is only the form of the body (Averroes). According to others (Fechner), who believed that not only man but also all organic and inorganic entities and even the whole universe is endowed with spirit, the human soul after death loses its individual being as a matter of fact, but does not perish, it merges itself into the soul of the universe as a drop of rain that falls into the sea.

## Religious metaphysics and ethics

The philosophical problems arising from religion that have been discussed above are in fact included in metaphysics but they are usually not indifferent to another philosophical discipline, namely normative ethics. Searching for answers to its fundamental questions: 'what is worth striving for?' and 'how should we guide our conduct?' many philosophers found the materials for these answers in the solutions to just such religio-philosophical problems. For some philosophers belief in God as the legislator of the moral world pointed out what man's moral obligations are, belief in the immortality of the soul has influenced opinions about that in which we should seek true happiness. Among the metaphysical problems whose solution, according to some, was required by ethics is also to be found the problem of the freedom of the will of which we spoke in relation to the problem of determinism. These three problems: the problem of God, of the immortality of the soul and of the freedom of the will, are considered by many to be the cardinal themes of metaphysical speculation. By pointing out the relation between these problems and normative ethics we should emphasise, in order to avoid misunderstanding, that it is not the case that all solutions to ethical problems have to resort to the three metaphysical problems mentioned above. Only some of the authors who deal with ethics resort to these metaphysical considerations. Ethics which proceeds in this way is called metaphysical ethics. It should be emphasised that not all normative ethics is metaphysical ethics and, above all, that not all normative ethics is religious ethics. Ethics not based on metaphysical considerations is called independent ethics.

# 11

## *Metaphysics as the attempt to achieve an ultimate world-outlook*

In previous pages we have learnt about the main problems contained in metaphyiscs. The variety of these problems is so great that it is not easy to grasp what unifies them; it is not easy to give a single concise formula in answer to the question what metaphysics is in such a way that it would not restrict the scope of metaphysical problems too narrowly. Most commonly metaphysics is described as the discipline which attempts to provide a world-outlook. The term 'world-outlook' is one of those terms which are very frequently used but whose meaning is only vaguely grasped. It has a whole gamut of interpretations. In the course of our argument we shall follow one of these interpretations. We shall also attempt to synthesise the divergent themes which metaphysics is concerned with, and attempt to show what unites them and what explains the fact that these problems have been brought together by philosophers practising metaphysics. Ontology, which has no closer a relation to the other metaphysical problems than it has to other branches of knowledge, remains outside the scope of this synthesis. Let us turn to our exposition.

Among things which we love, worship and respect there are

those to which we are attached, not because they possess particular qualities, but because we give our hearts to them regardless of their qualities. We love our native city, not because it is beautiful and inhabited by wonderful people, or because it has a noble history, we love it simply for nothing and nothing will reduce our devotion to it, even if we come to know other cities that are more wonderful than ours. We love our mothers not because of their virtues and we love them even more devotedly if when compared to others they lack beauty, charm, social grace, wisdom, housewifely skill or other qualities. A man in love is indifferent to other women's charms and he clings to the chosen one, not because she is more beautiful than others, but because she is herself.

Now apart from objects of love, worship and respect, loved and respected because they are what they are, there are objects which we respect because they possess certain qualities, and the respect we have for these objects is transferred immediately to other objects once we realise that it is the others that possess the qualities we had attributed to the original ones. And so, for instance, the admiration we had for the first automobiles created at the end of the nineteenth century and considered to be a miracle of technology we treat with condescension today when we compare them with the most recent models. As regards the second variety of our feelings towards objects, it clearly depends on the state of our knowledge and, first of all, on its extent. The inhabitants of a small town, who see nothing outside their little provincial world, honour and respect local celebrities to a degree they would never have reached had their horizons been wider and their scale of comparison more extensive. In the last analysis our evaluation of objects depends on our emotional attitude to them. Since this emotional attitude towards objects depends in many cases on our knowledge, the way we evaluate this or that is therefore also dependent on it.

Among different evaluations which we give, two are most

important. One is concerned with the value we attach to objects when we consider them from the point of view of their capacity for bringing us happiness. This kind of evaluation is called eudaemonic (from the Greek *eudaimonia* = happiness). The second kind of evaluation we have in mind is that of the moral evaluations which we give in recognising certain behaviour as right, as proper, as in agreement with our duty, as in agreement with our obligations. Now the evaluations that we give from these two points of view depend on the state of our knowledge, on its extent, on our horizons. A person from a small village would perceive as happiness something which he would consider as entirely unworthy of his efforts when he gets out into the world at large. A solicitous mother, for whom the world is confined by her own home and family, finds her duties limited to the care of her husband and children. It would not have occurred to her that somewhere else, possibly in the neighbourhood, orphans live who are deteriorating under neglect and who could be rescued from physical and moral ruin if a solicitous mother could give them some of her time and care without detriment to her own family. In behaving as she does she thinks she is doing what she ought to be doing, is fulfilling her duties. She would, however, have changed the evaluation of her behaviour had her thought-horizons been broadened, if the boundaries of the world in which she lives had been extended. These simple examples perhaps suffice to support the thesis that both our eudaemonic and moral evaluations depend in specific circumstances on the breadth of our horizons.

But the problem of eudaemonic evaluation as well as the problem of moral evaluation are too important to be rashly pronounced on by someone with narrow and confined horizons. Giving evaluations of these kinds in such circumstances, we risk having to change them when our horizons are broadened. So it is understandable that serious-minded people try to embrace such a large horizon by their thought that its breadth would guarantee that eudaemonic and moral evaluations based on it will not have to be changed when this horizon is extended. We shall call the totality of information contained in our thought-horizon which exerts a decisive influence on our eudaemonic and moral evaluation our world-view. As long as this world-view is provincial, evaluations based on it are provisional and may be changed with its expansion. Serious-minded people therefore try to ensure that their horizons are not provincial but rather that their world-view is complete.

In the history of European culture most people have found this ultimate world-view in religion. Religion maintains that all world-views excluding the after-life are limited. It itself, however, claims that it provides an ultimate world-view; ultimate in the sense that eudaemonic and moral evaluations based on it are unshakeable and need not fear change when our horizons are expanded. Religion thus satisfies the believer's need for an ultimate and not merely provincial and limited world-view. Whoever subscribes to a religion has a signpost in life which he is not going to reject as long as he adheres to his religion and regardless of whether the further progress of knowledge unveils for him horizons previously unknown.

Most believers gain their faith not by way of their own reflection or by means of personal experiences but accept it from the older generation in a way which is called in psychology 'suggestion of beliefs'.

One is brought up in a religion, that is to say religious beliefs are implanted in a human being from early childhood, together with a conviction that any doubt about their rightness is a sin. Only a few men base their religious beliefs on rational argument or on mystical experiences. Because of this, religious beliefs are shaken in many people from the age at which they begin to think independently and critically.

Along with this upheaval of their faith, their signpost towards ultimate happiness and duty, which is based on this belief, is also shaken. The need to find a new signpost brings with it the need to find, by one's own intellectual efforts, an ultimate world-view which would show what ultimate happiness and duty consist in. A large part of metaphysical problems arise from this striving directly or indirectly.

It is in this way that metaphysics emerged in the history of European thought in ancient Greece when at the beginning of the Hellenistic epoch faith in the Olympian gods collapsed and with it the authority of its commandments. It emerged with the task of finding foundations for moral and eudaemonic evaluation that were based not on tradition but on rational argument, the ultimate foundations which would provide an unalterable signpost in our striving for happiness and moral goodness.

Metaphysics thus emerged as an heir of religion. It inherited from it the task of creating an ultimate world-view but it proposed to arrive at it in a different way from that followed by religion, it proposed to base this world-view on independent inquiries of men.

So it is not surprising that metaphysics started first of all with religious theses which were meant to constitute this ultimate world-view. For many centuries religious problems – God, the immortality of the soul, the freedom of the will – constituted the core of metaphysical speculations, sometimes supporting the theses of the prevailing Christian religion and often rejecting them.

Reflection on the problem of the immortality of the soul directed the attention of metaphysicians towards the problem of the soul in general, that is to the question, what is it and whether, in general, anything of the kind exists. The problem of the freedom of the will prompted metaphysicians to consider the problem of determinism in general and thus the problem of causality. In this way the group of problems which we discussed under the heading 'problems arising from the investigation of nature' is connected with the group of problems arising from religion. Also connected with them is the problem of teleology, because this problem in its anthropomorphic form is rather closely connected with the problem of a personal Deity whose existence is evidenced by the purposive arrangement of the world. This problem is also, but in a different way, connected with the metaphysical search for a firm foundation for moral behaviour. The world as purposively arranged is the world in which every component has its role to carry out, has its destiny. Thus the suggestion occurs of considering as moral, that is as proper and just, that behaviour of man which is in accord with his destiny. Consequently the search for a moral signpost may be transformed into a search for the destiny of man, a search for the role which he has to play in the grand plan of creation. Search for this role leads directly into a search for the plan of the whole, of the aim or the sense of the world.

The metaphysician who strives towards an ultimate world-view tries to embrace a horizon so extensive that it could not be objected that recommendations based on this view, its paths of happiness and duty, are not provisional and will survive any broadening of horizons. But at his side the exact sciences reveal a rich and extensive picture of the world. The exact sciences, based on experience, penetrate nature more and more deeply. Is the metaphysician in his search for an ultimate world-view to become the conscientious pupil of natural scientists? Is he to learn a world-view from them?

Before the metaphysician who does not wish to be a provincial sage answers this question, he would like to know whether the world whose picture the natural sciences reveal to him constitutes the true reality and whether it is the only reality. The point is that another related philosophical discipline, the theory of knowledge, by analysing the problem of the sources of knowledge, sometimes arrives at conclusions from which it seems to follow that, apart from the experiential world, there exists another world of ideal objects, the world of ideas, truer and more genuine than the former. Reflecting on the limits of knowledge, and particularly of the knowledge based on experience which we rely on in the natural sciences, the theory of knowledge sometimes arrives at idealistic conclusions and these consequences cast a shadow on the genuineness of the reality of nature and prompt us to search for true reality beyond it. Therefore the metaphysician does not want to trust natural science blindly before he considers the problems that the theory of knowledge is concerned with and that may inspire a doubt that there may not be another world, the world of ideas or the world of things in themselves or whatever we choose to call them. If this were the case, as Platonic idealists or phenomenologists assert, doubt would arise as to whether the world-view based on the investigations of the natural sciences alone could be the kind of world-view the metaphysician is in search of; whether it would be an ultimate world-view, in no fear of the widening of horizons, or whether it would be only a provincial world-view. So it is understandable that the metaphysician also includes some epistemological problems in the programme of his investigations because the conclusions that follow from them will indicate to him whether the ultimate world-view he is seeking is to be learnt from investigators who apply the method of experience or whether he should look for it independently of them and by applying different methods from the ones they apply.

Depending on the position adopted in the theory of knowledge, the metaphysician will therefore be seeking his world-view in scientific knowledge or beyond it. If he takes an empiricist position in regard to the source of knowledge and a realist one in regard to the limits of knowledge, he will see no need or even possibility of seeking another world-view than the one provided by science as based on experience. If he inclines towards an aprioristic position, or even more if he is convinced by the arguments of irrationalists, he will seek his world-view in an aprioristic way, or he will appeal to intuition or mystical experiences. It is clear, therefore, that within the range of problems analysed by metaphysics some conclusions must be found which are derived from reflection upon knowledge and which were distinguished as a separate group of metaphysical considerations.

In these remarks we have tried to trace a thread connecting the problems discussed in this chapter with other metaphysical problems. We have tried to treat metaphysics as an attempt to embrace horizons large enough for eudaemonic and moral norms based on them not to fear revision when these horizons are further enlarged. We called the embracing of such horizons the attainment of an ultimate world-view. By describing metaphysics in this way we have tried to show that by treating it in this manner we can include in it the main groups of metaphysical problems which we discussed in detail in earlier chapters.

We are fully aware of the very general nature of the considerations which enter into this synthesis. It seems that in this matter it is hard to obtain anything more solid. There are numerous other attempts to describe metaphysics. Some of them are even more general than the description we have provided. Others are more precise, however they are not adequate to embrace the whole repertory of traditional problems contained in metaphysics, they consist more of a programme of investigations than of an attempt at a synthesis of existing investigations. We should add that in the remarks devoted to the description of metaphysics we have used the term 'world-view' in a more or less specific sense. It should be emphasised that this is not the only sense attached to this term by those who use it; the term is very general, ambiguous and vague and it can be made precise in different ways. We have chosen one of many.

The attempted synthesis of metaphysical problems provided here possesses, along with many drawbacks and vices, at any rate this merit: it shows the connections that obtain between the three basic philosophical disciplines – metaphysics, theory of knowledge and ethics. So it does introduce a certain unity into philosophy, which is considered by some to be a conglomerate of unconnected disciplines.

# Concluding Remarks

In the preceding chapters we have reviewed the problems which belong to metaphysics. At the same time we have systematised these problems to a certain extent and divided them into four groups: (1) the group of ontological problems; (2) the group of problems concerning the mode of existence of nature (arising from reflection about knowledge); (3) the group of problems concerning the substance and structure of the world (arising from reflection about nature); and (4) the group of problems arising from the need to adopt a position towards religious belief. Not all authors writing about metaphysics would agree with such a broadly circumscribed scope for it. Many authors understand metaphysics more narrowly than we have. This is expressed in numerous ways of describing metaphysics that are to be found in philosophical literature. The authors of these descriptions often confine metaphysics to only one of our four groups of problems and they adapt their definition to such a narrowly confined scope of the term 'metaphysics'. They do not include in metaphysics other groups of problems but relegate them to separate disciplines to which they give different names. In relation to all these ways of circumscribing the scope of metaphysical problems we have taken the most liberal course, including in metaphysics all the more important problems which can be subsumed under the term 'metaphysics', but without deviating too radically from the common use of the term. The motive behind this liberal treatment has been the desire to give the reader comprehensive information about the most important problems in a certain part of philosophy about whose name there is no uniform opinion. It may be that it would be appropriate to divide this group of problems which we included in one discipline – calling it metaphysics – into several different disciplines with distinctly circumscribed objects and ends. Such a division is suggested by the difficulty of finding one homogeneous description of the subject-matter and ends of metaphysics which would embrace equally well all the problems that have been included by us in metaphysics. The only description of metaphysics which suggests itself, as the discipline which is to provide a world-outlook, is – because of the vagueness of the term 'world-outlook' – too general and too little informative. On the other hand, the argument in favour of combining all these disciplines that we have mentioned into a whole as a single discipline is the relation in which these problems stand to each other. Indeed often problems that we have included in different groups are so tightly bound up with each other that the mode of solving one of them decides the standpoint from which the other is to be approached.

However, we have not considered it our task to provide a proper classification of philosophical problems. Our concern has only been to acquaint the reader with the content of these problems and with the main ways in which they may be solved.